I0605469

TO:
FROM:
DATE:

Rise and Renew

ONE STEP CLOSER

Rise and Renew

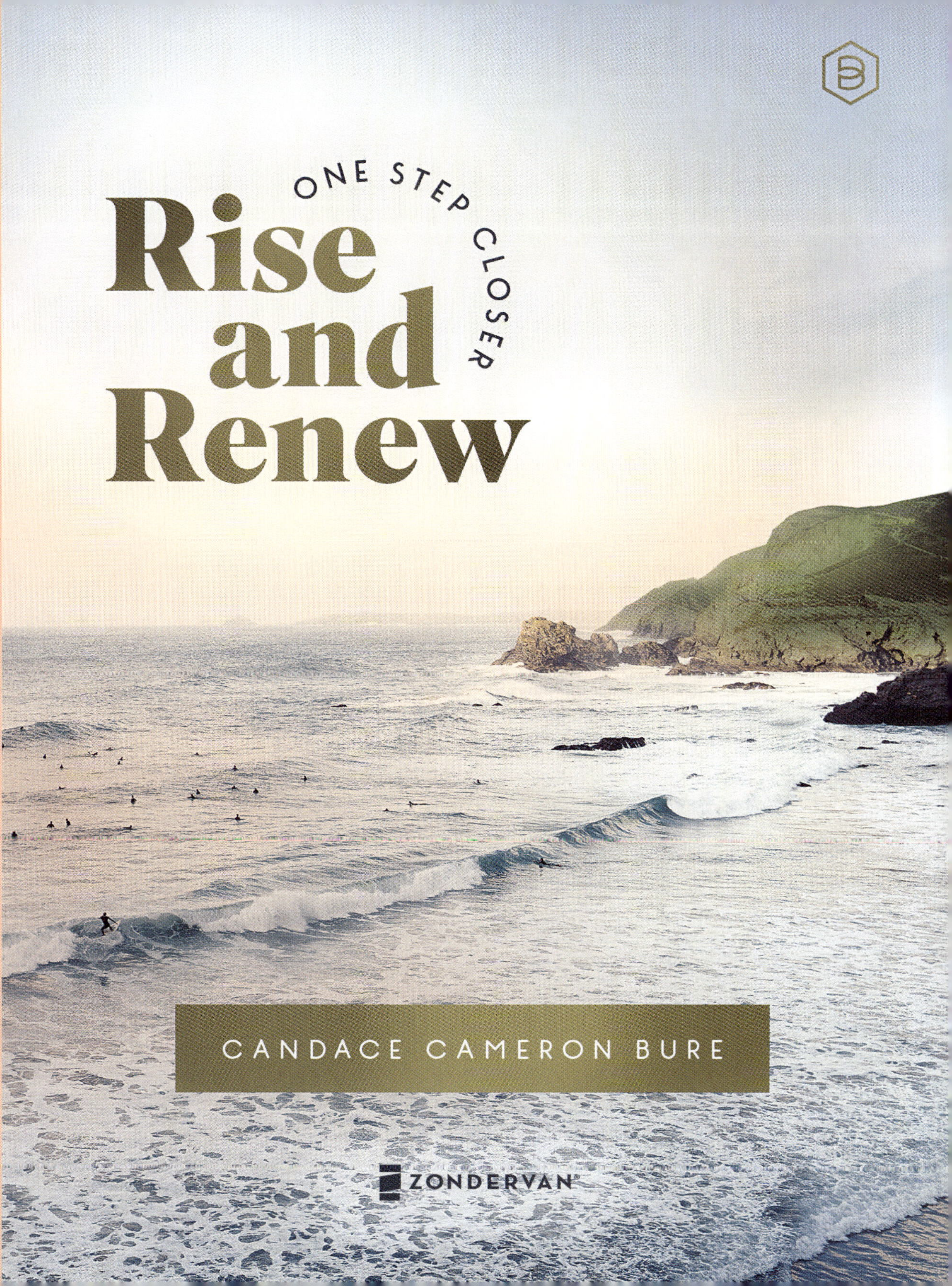

CANDACE CAMERON BURE

ZONDERVAN

ZONDERVAN

Rise and Renew

Published in Grand Rapids, Michigan, by Zondervan. Zondervan is a registered trademark of The Zondervan Corporation, L.L.C., a wholly owned subsidiary of HarperCollins Christian Publishing, Inc.

Requests for information should be addressed to customercare@harpercollins.com.

ISBN 978-0-310-46640-6 (HC)

Additional content collaboration: Christin Ditchfield
Art direction: Tiffany Forrester
Cover and interior design: Kathy Mitchell

Printed in India

25 26 27 28 29 REP 10 9 8 7 6 5 4 3

Contents

A NOTE FROM *Candace*

INTRODUCTION

At one time or another, every one of us has come face-to-face with our brokenness. On some level, we've all discovered that we're a hot mess—a bundle of contradictions, conflicting emotions, competing hopes, dreams, and desires. We look around us, we look in our own mirrors, and we measure ourselves by what seem like impossible standards—God's, our own, others'—only to find that we consistently come up short.

From my own life and the stories of others, I'm convinced that—although we have our shining moments—many of us wrestle with this brokenness daily. We battle feelings of guilt and failure and frustration, feelings of unworthiness, hopelessness, and despair.

And with each new day, each new challenge or opportunity, we question ourselves:

- What if we just can't do this?
- What if we fall?
- What if we fail?

But I believe there are better questions we can ask:

- What if our brokenness doesn't define us? What if we let go of our past failures and mistakes, let go of the pain, and rise up to overcome the challenges before us and live out the calling God gives us?
- What if we try?
- What if we fly?

God says we can. We can soar in the power of His Spirit! He says He is with us and He is for us. His love for us will never fail. His mercies are new every morning.

He will not let us fall.

God says He loves us just as we are—in all our brokenness—but He loves us too much to leave us this way. He has something better for us than brokenness. He offers us redemption, hope, and healing.

God calls us to rise and renew:

> Since you have heard about Jesus and have learned the truth that comes from him, throw off your old sinful nature and your former way of life. . . . Instead, let the Spirit renew your thoughts and attitudes. Put on your new nature, created to be like God—truly righteous and holy. (Ephesians 4:21–24)

Colossians 3:10 describes this new nature as "a fresh new you, which is continually renewed in knowledge according to the image of the One who created you" (THE VOICE).

You and I, we can do this. With God's help, we can live in this "newness of life," this wholeness and healing, every single day (Romans 6:4 NKJV).

You may be saying, "Candace, I want to experience this! I want to answer God's call to rise and renew. But I don't know what that looks like, where to start, or what to do."

What if, for thirty days, we discover together what it means to rise and renew? Whether you spread out that process over several weeks or do it for thirty days straight, let's team up!

To get us one step closer to that goal of becoming the spiritually whole and healthy women we've been created to be, we have packed thirty days' worth of inspiration inside these pages. That means you can begin today! You don't need a seminary degree or a church background to join me. You don't even have to own a Bible. Just bring along something to write with and a willing spirit, and you're covered. This devotional guide is equipped with the encouragement you need to succeed: the power of Scripture, a devotional reading from my heart to yours, guided questions where we can clarify the challenges each of us is facing, and lots of creative exercises for taking action to overcome them! Together we will discover some of the many ways God calls us to rise and renew. The more we focus our hearts and minds on His truths, the more we will be inspired and empowered to answer His call.

The Bible tells us that God gives us "a crown of beauty instead of ashes, the oil of joy instead of mourning, and a garment of praise instead of a spirit of despair" (Isaiah 61:3 NIV). We don't have to stay broken, because we have His Spirit living in us and working through us. We have His healing love giving us a hope and a courage and a confidence that nothing can shake. Friend, we can be redeemed. We can be made new. We can rise and renew.

Let's start *today*!

In this together,

Candace

A QUICK Q&A FROM CANDACE

Wherever you are on your spiritual journey, I want you to know you're not alone. We all have questions about God and faith, so I've answered some questions people typically ask me about my Christian faith. I hope these answers will be helpful to you too.

WHY SHOULD I READ AND STUDY THE BIBLE?

The Bible is full of history, wisdom, guidelines, and poetry, but as a whole, it's actually the epic story about all of creation and time from the beginning to the end. In the Bible, God is the ultimate Storyteller—He shares His plan, His story, and His design for the world and for humanity. No other book is so transformational because no other book shows us how much we are loved by our Creator.

WHAT DOES IT MEAN TO BE "SAVED"?

When followers of Jesus talk about being saved, we mean that Jesus rescued us from the ultimate consequence of sin—eternal separation from God. When we continually choose our way rather than God's way, we become filled with darkness, hopelessness, shame, guilt, and fear. Being "saved" means we acknowledge that Jesus is the Way and that He shines His light, freedom, joy, peace, and hope into our lives.

WHAT IF I DON'T THINK I NEED TO BE SAVED?

I get this too—you're a good person and you're not hurting anyone. Why do you need to be saved, right? We have to realize that God's standards are different from human standards. If we just compare ourselves to other people, it's easy to think we're good enough. But when we compare ourselves to God's standards, we fall miserably short. Every. Single. Time. But because God loves us, He sent His Son, Jesus, to die so that all people—no matter what they've done or where they come from—could be fully forgiven and have a loving relationship with Him.

IS THERE REALLY ONLY ONE WAY TO GOD?

This is a tough one for a lot of people, but the short answer is yes. There is only one way to God, and it's through Jesus Christ. Jesus didn't say, "I am one of the ways to God." Jesus said, "I am the way, the truth, and the life. No one can come to the Father except through me" (John 14:6). He's it. He's the only way.

Though this idea may seem narrow, it's actually quite comforting. Many religions teach people to work to earn their right standing with God. With Jesus, being right with God doesn't depend on what we do or don't do. It depends on what Jesus has already done: He died on the cross to take the punishment for our sins, and then He rose again to give us life with Him. All we have to do is acknowledge our sinfulness, ask God for His forgiveness, and then accept His gift of salvation. Then we get to spend our lives loving Him.

HOW CAN I HAVE A RELATIONSHIP WITH GOD?

If you ask God how to find Him, He will make it very clear to you. One way to strengthen your bond with your heavenly Father is simply to talk to Him—tell Him your worries, fears, concerns, doubts, hopes, and dreams. Tell Him all of it! Prayer doesn't need to be long or eloquent. Physical posture or volume doesn't make prayer more or less effective. God say that when you pray, "be sure that your faith is in God alone" (James 1:6).

As you pray, listen for God's voice. How do you know when God is speaking to you? God speaks to us in different ways, and He'll never say something that contradicts what the Bible teaches. When I'm reading certain verses and my heart does something like a flip-flop, I know that God is showing me something important and I need to pay attention.

God will also speak to us through friends, pastors, and teachers. He may even reveal Himself to us through nature or certain circumstances. Just be open to however He wants to speak to you.

HOW DO I USE THIS DEVOTIONAL GUIDE?

I love this devotional guide because it encourages you to experience the life-changing message of God's Word for yourself. Each of the thirty entries includes the following:

- **Scripture Passages**

  Each entry starts with what God says about His call to rise and renew. Be sure to read each verse, say the words out loud, and maybe even memorize them so you can repeat them back to yourself whenever you need to renew your heart, your mind, and your strength.

- **A Note from Candace**

  I love telling people about the many ways God has redeemed and restored my life. I'm sharing some of the real-life moments when I've leaned on my Savior for help and hope and healing to remind you that God wants to help you and heal you too. We really can be made new! It's taken me a long time to understand this (and let's face it, I still forget a lot), but it's true! God's got this!

- **Think on It**

  Your turn! It's time to answer a few reflection questions about where you are in life, how you're feeling, and who you are becoming. Sometimes answers will come quickly, and sometimes you may have to do some soul searching, but either way, the exercise of writing down your answers will help you acknowledge and focus on where you are in your spiritual journey. Be honest! This is your safe space.

- **Act on It**

  I want you to think outside of the box, so every entry includes a different interactive activity such as making a list, drawing, writing out prayers, and more—all ways to help you find a fresh, new perspective on the topic at hand.

I hope that through this thirty-day journey—through the Scripture passages, testimonies, questions, and activities—you'll find yourself letting go of the past and looking forward to the glorious future God has prepared for you! You'll rise up with fresh courage and strength and hope, believing that God is making all things new, including you.

ONLINE COMPANION COURSE

Want more? I created an online companion course for you! Scan the QR code with a mobile device to see how you can join me for exclusive Scripture readings, stories, and a community where you can connect with other readers.

LET'S DO THIS!

I'm thrilled that we are embarking on this journey together. We are about to learn how to move beyond our brokenness and into the new life God promises us. Yes, our brokenness is real, but so is our hope and so is God's help and healing. God says He has redeemed us and restored us (Ephesians 1:7–8). We don't have to stay stuck in the pain of our past. We don't have to live in discouragement and defeat. Each and every day, we can rise up and renew our strength, we can be renewed by the power of His Spirit working in us and through us.

Before we get started, let's all say this little prayer and ask God to be with us in the process:

> *Dear God, be with me during this thirty-day journey. I want to be closer to You. You know, Lord, that sometimes I get disappointed and discouraged. I feel weary and worn out, frustrated and helpless. I want to find courage and strength. I want to find hope and healing. Help me to believe that You are with me, that You love me, and that You will redeem and restore every part of me. Show me what I need to learn to grow closer to You, shine Your light on the topics in this book that I need to dive deeper into, and each day help me to answer Your call to rise up and renew. In Jesus' name, amen.*

Day
1

Rise Up *in* Redemption

Stand up and lift up your heads, because your redemption is drawing near.

LUKE 21:28 NIV

Praise be to the God and Father of our Lord Jesus Christ, who has blessed us in the heavenly realms with every spiritual blessing in Christ.

EPHESIANS 1:3 NIV

Colossians 1:13–14 *NIV*	For he has rescued us from the dominion of darkness and brought us into the kingdom of the Son he loves, in whom we have redemption, the forgiveness of sins.
Romans 6:4	For we died and were buried with Christ by baptism. And just as Christ was raised from the dead by the glorious power of the Father, now we also may live new lives.
1 Corinthians 12:12–13 *THE MESSAGE*	Each of us is now a part of his resurrection body, refreshed and sustained at one fountain—his Spirit—where we all come to drink.
Psalm 107:1–2 *THE MESSAGE*	Oh, thank GOD—he's so good! His love never runs out. All of you set free by GOD, tell the world!
Psalm 107:2	Has the LORD redeemed you? Then speak out! Tell others.
Psalm 103:2–5	Let all that I am praise the LORD; may I never forget the good things he does for me. He forgives all my sins and heals all my diseases. He redeems me from death and crowns me with love and tender mercies. He fills my life with good things.
Lamentations 3:58 *AMP*	O Lord, You have pleaded my soul's cause [You have guided my way and protected me]; You have rescued and redeemed my life.
Psalm 146:1	Praise the LORD! Let all that I am praise the LORD.

A NOTE FROM *Candace*

Rise Up in Redemption

I've often heard it said, "We're Easter people living in a Good Friday world."

The world we live in is full of chaos. Full of sin. Full of brokenness, hurt, and heartache. Pain and frustration. Division and conflict. Disappointment and despair. Hopelessness and helplessness—just about everywhere.

But into all this brokenness came Jesus.

Into this darkness came the Light.

What glorious good news!

The Bible tells us that Jesus suffered and died to deliver us from evil. To rescue us. To redeem us. That's what Good Friday is all about. It's why we call it *good*—even when it commemorates His horrific death.

Because it was good for us. We desperately needed that redemption.

To *redeem* someone is to save them—or to atone for their failures and mistakes. To make amends on their behalf. To pay their debt. To buy them back from slavery. To purchase their freedom.

And that's exactly what Jesus has done for us.

But death had no claim on Him—no right to hold Him. It couldn't keep Him in the grave.

So Jesus rose from the dead, in power and glory. He lives!

That's what Easter is all about.

The Bible tells us that the same power that raised Jesus from the dead lives in us—the same Spirit. And that Spirit is at work even now, constantly and continually redeeming us, resurrecting us, and restoring us.

Giving us the courage and the grace and the strength to rise up and renew.

One day the restoration, the renewal, will be complete. Once and for all, we will be fully healed. Resurrected. Transformed. Set free. Forever and ever. Amen.

Until then, we live in the tension between what we once were, what we are, and what we will be.

But we don't live in this place alone. Even here, He is with us.

And that's the best news of all, for you and for me.

think on it

What drew you to this devotional guide—to this thirty-day journey?

What do you think of when you hear the phrase "rise and renew"? What about it speaks to you?

Where in your life do you long to rise up in the power of God's Spirit?

think on it

Where in your life would you like to experience renewal?

In 1 Corinthians 1:30, it says, "Everything that we have—right thinking and right living, a clean slate and a fresh start—comes from God by way of Jesus Christ" (THE MESSAGE). How do these words challenge, encourage, or inspire you?

What questions do you have as we begin our journey? What do you hope to learn?

Act on It

Take a few moments right now to write a prayer in your own words, from your heart to God's, sharing the things you've been thinking about, thanking Him for meeting you here, asking Him to be with you on this journey and to give you the courage, the grace, and the power to rise and renew:

HOPE IN THE LORD; FOR WITH THE LORD THERE IS UNFAILING LOVE. HIS REDEMPTION OVERFLOWS.

PSALM 130:7

Day
2

Rise Up *in* Forgiveness

When we were utterly helpless, Christ came at just the right time and died for us sinners.

ROMANS 5:6

I want you to know, my very dear friends, that it is on account of this resurrected Jesus that the forgiveness of your sins can be promised. . . . Everyone who believes in this raised-up Jesus is declared good and right and whole before God.

ACTS 13:38–39 THE MESSAGE

Romans 6:9–11
THE MESSAGE

Our old way of life was nailed to the cross with Christ, a decisive end to that sin-miserable life—no longer captive to sin's demands! What we believe is this: If we get included in Christ's sin-conquering death, we also get included in his life-saving resurrection. We know that when Jesus was raised from the dead it was a signal of the end of death-as-the-end. Never again will death have the last word. When Jesus died, he took sin down with him, but alive he brings God down to us. From now on, think of it this way: Sin speaks a dead language that means nothing to you; God speaks your mother tongue, and you hang on every word. You are dead to sin and alive to God. That's what Jesus did.

Romans 8:1
THE VOICE

Therefore, now no condemnation awaits those who are living in Jesus the Anointed, *the Liberating King*.

1 John 1:9
AMP

If we [freely] admit that we have sinned *and* confess our sins, He is faithful and just [true to His own nature and promises], and will forgive our sins and cleanse us *continually* from all unrighteousness [our wrongdoing, everything not in conformity with His will and purpose].

Psalm 86:5

O Lord, you are so good, so ready to forgive, so full of unfailing love for all who ask for your help.

Psalm 65:3

Though we are overwhelmed by our sins, you forgive them all.

Rise Up in Forgiveness

There's so much more to our story than our brokenness. Because of Jesus, we have forgiveness. We have hope. We have healing. We have freedom!

The Bible tells us we have an Enemy who is actively trying to tear us down, tear us apart. He wants to discourage and defeat us. He pours on the guilt and shame and the condemnation. He reminds us constantly of our brokenness, of our past failures and mistakes. He'd like nothing more than to see us curled up in a ball, conquered and cowering.

But Jesus calls to us, "Rise up" (Ephesians 5:14).

He calls us to stand tall—stand in His mercy and His grace, His love and His forgiveness.

Believe what He has done for us.

Receive all that He has for us.

Live in the rich and deep abundance—the fullness of life—that He gave us by giving up His own life.

No matter how our Enemy tries to distract us or deceive us, we hold fast to the truth.

We hold on tight—we cling—to Jesus.

We keep our eyes on Him.

And as we stand there, looking at Him, we find Him looking at us—with all the love in the world. All the tenderness and compassion. Understanding.

No condemnation (Romans 8:1). Forgiveness—it's who He is. Forgiven—that's who we are in Him.

How have you experienced forgiveness? What does it look like or feel like? What does it mean to you?

The Bible calls the Enemy of our souls "a liar" (John 8:44). How can you resist him when he tries to discourage you or defeat you? What truths can you hold on to?

think on it

How can you rise up in forgiveness today? What will you say to yourself about yourself?

In Luke 11:4, Jesus taught us to pray, "Forgive us our sins, as we forgive those who sin against us." He wants us to be like Him—to love and forgive others the way He has loved and forgiven us. It's not always easy, but He promises to help us. Who do you need to forgive today?

Act on It

Colossians 2:13–14 says, "When you were stuck in your old sin-dead life, you were incapable of responding to God. God brought you alive—right along with Christ! Think of it! All sins forgiven, the slate wiped clean, that old arrest warrant canceled and nailed to Christ's cross" (THE MESSAGE).

Take a few moments right now to confess any sin that's been weighing on you, any guilt and shame you've been carrying. Write it down—and then depending on the way you've chosen to record this confession, you can actually or symbolically . . .

Tear it up.
Burn it.
Bury it.
Drop it.
Wash it away.
Blot it out.
White it out.
Erase it.
Nail it to a cross.

The Bible uses all of this language—this imagery—to try to help us understand what God has done with our sin, what His forgiveness means.

Now rise up and thank Him! Praise Him! Bless His holy name!

IF YOU, LORD, KEPT A RECORD OF SINS, LORD, WHO COULD STAND? BUT WITH YOU THERE IS FORGIVENESS.

PSALM 130:3–4 NIV

Day
3

Rise Up *in* Hope

Anyone who belongs to Christ has become a new person. The old life is gone; a new life has begun!

2 CORINTHIANS 5:17

May you have the power to understand, as all God's people should, how wide, how long, how high, and how deep his love is.

EPHESIANS 3:18

Ephesians 3:19
AMP

[That you may come] to know [practically, through personal experience] the love of Christ which far surpasses [mere] knowledge [without experience], that you may be filled up [throughout your being] to all the fullness of God [so that you may have the richest experience of God's presence in your lives, completely filled and flooded with God Himself].

Ephesians 4:23
THE MESSAGE

And then take on an entirely new way of life—a God-fashioned life, a life renewed from the inside and working itself into your conduct as God accurately reproduces his character in you.

Colossians 3:10–11

Put on your new nature, and be renewed as you learn to know your Creator and become like him. In this new life . . . Christ is all that matters, and he lives in all of us.

1 Peter 4:19

Keep on doing what is right, and trust your lives to the God who created you, for he will never fail you.

Ephesians 3:20
THE MESSAGE

God can do anything, you know—far more than you could ever imagine or guess or request in your wildest dreams!

A NOTE FROM *Candace*

Rise Up in Hope

Many people think I grew up in a Christian home, but I didn't. I grew up in a moral home, a home that stressed the importance of living by the golden rule. But it wasn't until my parents hit a hard place in their marriage that the four of us kids found ourselves in church. I was twelve years old.

For the longest time, my dad wasn't interested.

My mom was finding all kinds of hope and joy in her faith. She was rising up and being renewed—growing and thriving spiritually.

But my dad said, "No thanks. Not for me."

For more than thirty years, whenever she invited him to church or tried to start conversations about spiritual things, that was his answer.

But hope is a powerful thing.

Especially when that hope is in Jesus.

Hope says the story isn't finished—it's only just begun. "So be truly glad. There is wonderful joy ahead" (1 Peter 1:6).

There are miracles coming, answers to prayer on the way.

"The faithful love of the LORD never ends! His mercies never cease. Great is his faithfulness; his mercies begin afresh each morning" (Lamentations 3:22–23).

So rise up!

Mom rose up in hope, day after day, year after year. She kept hoping, kept believing, kept trusting, kept praying that one day my dad, too, would rise up in hope and be made new.

And one day it happened—he did. He has. He teaches Bible studies and volunteers in prison ministry today.

Rising up in hope changes everything.

think on it

What does rising up in hope mean to you?

What are you hoping for? Whom are you hoping in?

In 1 Thessalonians 1:2–3, it says, "Every time we think of you, we thank God for you. Day and night you're in our prayers as we call to mind your work of faith, your labor of love, and your patience of hope in following our Master, Jesus Christ" (THE MESSAGE). Where is God calling you to be patient in hope today?

think on it

Isaiah 40:31 says, "But those who wait for the Lord [who expect, look for, and hope in Him] will gain new strength *and* renew their power; they will lift up their wings [and rise up close to God] like eagles [rising toward the sun]; they will run and not become weary, they will walk and not grow tired" (AMP). How does this word picture inspire you to rise up in hope while you wait?

Act on It

Take a few moments to affirm your hope and faith and trust in God today. Create your own "I believe" declaration. If you need a little help to get started, you can use some of these prompts:

I believe that God . . .

I believe that I . . .

I believe that this life . . .

I believe that right now . . .

I believe that one day . . .

I live in hope that . . .

I live in hope because . . .

I rise up in . . .

THIS I DECLARE ABOUT THE LORD. . . . HE IS MY GOD, AND I TRUST HIM.

PSALM 91:2

Day
4

Rise Up *in* Healing

Eternal One, my True God, I cried out to You for help;
You mended the shattered pieces of my life.

PSALM 30:2 THE VOICE

O Lord my God, I cried to you for help, and you restored my health.

PSALM 30:2

Isaiah 61:1–7
THE MESSAGE

The Spirit of GOD, the Master, is on me because GOD anointed me. He sent me to preach good news to the poor, heal the heartbroken, announce freedom to all captives, pardon all prisoners. GOD sent me to announce the year of his grace . . . and to comfort all who mourn, to care for the needs of all who mourn in Zion, give them bouquets of roses instead of ashes, messages of joy instead of news of doom, a praising heart instead of a languid spirit. Rename them "Oaks of Righteousness" planted by GOD to display his glory. They'll rebuild the old ruins, raise a new city out of the wreckage. They'll start over on the ruined cities, take the rubble left behind and make it new.

Malachi 4:2

For you who fear my name, the Sun of Righteousness will rise with healing in his wings.

1 Peter 2:24
AMP

He personally carried our sins in His body on the cross [willingly offering Himself on it, as on an altar of sacrifice], so that we might die to sin [becoming immune from the penalty and power of sin] and live for righteousness; for by His wounds you [who believe] have been healed.

Psalm 147:3

He heals the brokenhearted and bandages their wounds.

Ecclesiastes 3:11

God has made everything beautiful for its own time.

Rise Up in Healing

I absolutely, unequivocally believe in the miraculous and mighty power of God to raise us up, to redeem us, to restore us, and to heal us . . . and one day to resurrect us!

Because I've seen it. I've experienced it.

Through the power of His Holy Spirit, God has brought healing to my hurting heart time and time again. He has comforted me and strengthened me and sustained me in more ways than I can tell.

He's brought healing and renewal to my marriage. There were some dark days when I really didn't think we were going to make it, but God brought us through.

He has brought healing and renewal in other relationships too.

Some of my friends have experienced that healing with their children or their parents or other friends in situations that seemed unhealable.

Hopeless even.

But God . . .

God intervened. He stepped up and stepped in and did what only He can do. He helped them to rise and renew.

Some have had healing in their bodies, others in their hearts or minds or spirits.

Some have been healed on this side of eternity, others on the other side.

But all of us who call on His name, who run to Him, who put our hope and trust in Him—all of us have found that He is faithful. He is good and wise and kind, compassionate, tenderhearted, and loving toward all He has made.

There is no hopeless cause, no hopeless case. Nothing too difficult or complicated. Nothing that can't be helped, healed, redeemed, restored, or renewed.

Nothing is impossible for Him.

The Scripture says He gives "beauty for ashes" (Isaiah 61:3 NKJV). He takes the worst that life throws at us, the worst mess we can make of things, and somehow makes it all work together for our good (Romans 8:28).

In what areas have you been most aware of your own brokenness?

Where have you been hurt or wounded? Where are you in need of healing?

How have you experienced God's healing? What does it look like? How does it feel?

think on it

Where are you still waiting for (or, with God's help, working on) healing?

In 2 Corinthians 1:3–4, Paul exclaimed, "All praise to the God and Father of our Master, Jesus the Messiah! Father of all mercy! God of all healing counsel! He comes alongside us when we go through hard times, and before you know it, he brings us alongside someone else who is going through hard times so that we can be there for that person just as God was there for us" (THE MESSAGE). How have you experienced this? How have you received support and encouragement from others? How have you been helped in your healing?

How has God empowered you to give support and encouragement to others? How have you helped others in their healing?

Act on It

Find a picture that represents your life somehow—tear one out of a magazine or print one from your computer or phone. Cut it up into a few large pieces, representing the brokenness that you—that all of us—experience.

Now paste it back together in the space below as you reflect on God's healing work in your heart and life. You can add a little glitter to the seams—or strips of fabric, bandages, or stickers—or just doodle around the edges to embellish the image and represent how God transforms our brokenness into something beautiful.

GOD MADE MY LIFE COMPLETE WHEN I PLACED ALL THE PIECES BEFORE HIM.

PSALM 18:20 THE MESSAGE

Day
5

Rise Up *in* Courage

Be strong and courageous, all you who put your hope in the Lord!

PSALM 31:24

Don't be afraid, I've redeemed you. I've called your name. You're mine. When you're in over your head, I'll be there with you. When you're in rough waters, you will not go down. When you're between a rock and a hard place, it won't be a dead end—because I am God, your personal God, the Holy of Israel, your Savior.

ISAIAH 43:1–3 THE MESSAGE

Isaiah 57:15
THE MESSAGE

I live in the high and holy places, but also with the low-spirited, the spirit-crushed, and what I do is put new spirit in them, get them up and on their feet again.

Isaiah 57:15

I restore the crushed spirit of the humble and revive the courage of those with repentant hearts.

Isaiah 41:10

Don't be afraid, for I am with you. Don't be discouraged, for I am your God. I will strengthen you and help you. I will hold you up with my victorious right hand.

Joshua 1:9

This is my command—be strong and courageous! Do not be afraid or discouraged. For the LORD your God is with you wherever you go.

Isaiah 35:3–4
THE MESSAGE

Tell fearful souls, "Courage! Take heart! GOD is here, right here, on his way to put things right. . . . He's on his way! He'll save you!"

Hebrews 13:5 THE VOICE

I will never leave you; I will always be by your side.

Matthew 28:20

And be sure of this: I am with you always, even to the end of the age.

Rise Up in Courage

I wonder if we sometimes get a little too comfortable with our brokenness, maybe just a little too complacent about our failures and mistakes.

I think sometimes it feels easier just to stay in that place. It feels safer not to risk anything more. Safer not to even *try* to get up or to grow or to change.

It takes real courage to rise up and renew.

That's the truth.

It takes courage to face our fears, to overcome our failures, to learn and grow from our mistakes.

It takes courage to be willing to change. Courage to believe we *can* change. Courage to take steps toward change.

It takes courage to try and try again.

The good news is, we've got it! Courage, I mean.

That is, *God's* got it—all the courage we need—and He's ready and willing to give it to us each and every day.

He wants to fill us with His Spirit, make us bold and strong and courageous, help us be all that He has created us to be.

Even when we can't see it. Even when we don't feel it. Even if we're not sure how to start—or where.

He meets us right here, right now, in this time and place. In our heart of hearts. In our unspoken needs. Our deepest longings. Our secret dreams.

He tells us that He loves us so much more than we can possibly imagine. He says He wants only the very best for us. And He promises He will be with us.

He will take us by the hand, lift us up, and lead us every single step of the way.

So rise up. Take courage, dear heart!

Take all the courage He gives.

Receive all the courage you need.

think on it

What's the biggest fear you battle right now?

Where do you most need courage today?

What do you need courage to believe?

think on it

In Psalm 34:4, the psalmist said, "I prayed to the LORD, and he answered me. He freed me from all my fears." How has God given you courage in the past? What obstacles have you already faced—with His help—and overcome?

In 2 Timothy 1:7 it says God has *not* given us a spirit of fear, but one of "power, love, and self-discipline." Why is this so important to know? What difference does it make?

Psalm 56:3 says, "When I am afraid, I will put my trust *and* faith in You" (AMP). How can you do this today? What steps will you take to rise and renew?

Act on It

King David in the Bible faced all kinds of fierce enemies and more than his fair share of humiliating failures and mistakes. But he always, always found a way to rise and renew. He went to God again and again for courage and strength, for forgiveness and faith—and we can too!

In Psalm 27:1, David wrote, "The LORD is my light and my salvation; whom shall I fear? [T]he LORD is the strength of my life; of whom shall I be afraid?" (KJV).

Draw a candle below. Then in the "darkness" around it, write down any worries, doubts, or fears that are shadowing you. Then use a highlighter or colored pencil to flood them in light—the light that radiates from the risen Christ, the Light of the World, and your salvation!

TAKE COURAGE! FOR I BELIEVE GOD.
IT WILL BE JUST AS HE SAID.

ACTS 27:25

Day
6

Rise Up *in* Power

Now all glory to God, who is able, through his mighty power at work within us, to accomplish infinitely more than we might ask or think.

EPHESIANS 3:20

Be strong in the Lord and in his mighty power.

EPHESIANS 6:10

Romans 8:11	The Spirit of God, who raised Jesus from the dead, lives in you.
Isaiah 40:29	He gives power to the weak and strength to the powerless.
Romans 8:26	And the Holy Spirit helps us in our weakness.
Ephesians 3:16	I pray that from his glorious, unlimited resources he will empower you with inner strength through his Spirit.
2 Corinthians 4:7	We now have this light shining in our hearts, but we ourselves are like fragile clay jars containing this great treasure. This makes it clear that our great power is from God, not from ourselves.
2 Corinthians 12:9–10 THE MESSAGE	He told me, My grace is enough; it's all you need. My strength comes into its own in your weakness. Once I heard that. . . . I just let Christ take over! And so the weaker I get, the stronger I become.
2 Corinthians 4:16–17 THE MESSAGE	So we're not giving up. How could we! Even though on the outside it often looks like things are falling apart on us, on the inside, where God is making new life, not a day goes by without his unfolding grace.

A NOTE FROM
Candace

Rise Up in Power

The Bible talks a lot about God's power at work in us. It describes this power as "mighty" and "limitless"—able to accomplish "infinitely more than we might ask"—or as one translation of Ephesians 3:20 puts it, "superabundantly more than all that we dare ask or think [infinitely beyond our greatest prayers, hopes, or dreams]" (AMP).

I love this!

I spent so much of my life chasing my own dreams, striving to do things in my own strength and winding up exhausted, frustrated, and discouraged. Feeling helpless and hopeless. But when I learned that I could rely on God's power in me, my life began changing in amazing ways! I discovered new dreams—God's dreams, His plans and purposes. And I found new hope, new courage, new energy, and new strength to pursue them.

I learned then—and I'm still learning—that "I can do all things [which He has called me to do] through Him who strengthens *and* empowers me [to fulfill His purpose—I am self-sufficient in Christ's sufficiency; I am ready for anything and equal to anything through Him who infuses me with inner strength and confident peace]" (Philippians 4:13 AMP).

And when I am weak? That's when I'm strong—because He is strong! That's when His power is at work in me and through me.

When I struggle, when I stumble and fall, He catches me. When I cry out to Him, He helps me. He forgives me for my sin, for all my failures and mistakes. He heals me. He redeems me and restores me.

He raises me up in His strength. He renews me by His Spirit.

And I know He can do the same for you.

Our lives may look different—our circumstances, our responsibilities, the challenges and obstacles we face—but the same mighty God at work in me is also at work in you.

Your weakness—like mine—is just an opportunity for His power and His glory to shine through.

think on it

How have you experienced God's power in your life? Where have you seen His power working in you and through you? What have you accomplished in His strength that you know you couldn't have accomplished on your own?

What are the biggest challenges you face right now? What is God calling you to do?

When are you tempted to rely on your own strength?

think on it

Where do you feel weakest? What do you know you can't do without God's help—without His power and strength working in you?

Romans 8:26 tells us, "The Holy Spirit helps us in our weakness." The psalmist said, "As soon as I pray, you answer me; you encourage me by giving me strength" (Psalm 138:3). Take a few moments right now to ask God for His help today. Ask Him to give you the power you need to rise up in His strength, by His grace, and for His glory.

Act on It

It's God's Spirit working in us and through us that gives us the power to rise up and renew! Because of Him, we can do all kinds of things we would never have dared to dream or imagine. We can face life's challenges head-on, confident that He will give us victory.

Write a prayer below, asking God to help you face any upcoming challenges with confidence in Him.

Then grab a dumbbell (or a picture of one) and put it somewhere you will see it often this week. Every time you do, pause and ask God to fill you with His power and thank Him for all the strength He's already given you.

GOD ARMS ME WITH STRENGTH.

PSALM 18:32

Day
7

Rise Up *in* Faith

Hold on to the pattern of wholesome teaching you learned . . . a pattern shaped by the faith and love that you have in Christ Jesus.

2 TIMOTHY 1:13

Just as you accepted Christ Jesus as your Lord, you must continue to follow him. Let your roots grow down into him, and let your lives be built on him. Then your faith will grow strong in the truth you were taught, and you will overflow with thankfulness.

COLOSSIANS 2:6–7

1 Timothy 6:11 THE MESSAGE

Pursue a righteous life—a life of wonder, faith, love.

1 Timothy 1:19

Cling to your faith in Christ.

Hebrews 11:1
THE MESSAGE

The fundamental fact of existence is that this trust in God, this faith, is the firm foundation under everything that makes life worth living. It's our handle on what we can't see.

Romans 5:1–2
THE MESSAGE

By entering through faith into what God has always wanted to do for us—set us right with him, make us fit for him—we have it all together with God because of our Master Jesus. And that's not all: We throw open our doors to God and discover at the same moment that he has already thrown open his door to us. We find ourselves standing where we always hoped we might stand—out in the wide open spaces of God's grace and glory, standing tall and shouting our praise.

Ephesians 3:12

Because of Christ and our faith in him, we can now come boldly and confidently into God's presence.

Hebrews 4:16

So let us come boldly to the throne of our gracious God. There we will receive his mercy, and we will find grace to help us when we need it most.

A NOTE FROM *Candace*

Rise Up in Faith

Faith is believing that God is who He says He is—and that He does what He says He will do.

Faith is believing that we are loved, we are called, we are chosen, and we belong to Him.

Faith is believing that He forgives.

Faith is believing that we can start again. And again. As many times as it takes.

Faith reminds us that we are strong in His strength.

Faith says we can rise up and renew.

Faith carries us through.

Faith gives us hope.

Faith gives us a courage and confidence that nothing can shake us.

Faith builds our lives on the bedrock of God's truth.

Faith perseveres in the hard times, pushes through the dark times, keeps moving forward, step by step, day after day.

Faith moves mountains when we pray.

Faith makes space for miracles, watches them unfold, and celebrates!

Faith makes us bold.

Faith holds firm, fights hard, finishes strong.

Faith lives.

Faith is a gift.

How has your faith been a gift to you?

When did you first receive it?
What does it mean to you now?

In 1 Peter 1:6–7, it says, "Be truly glad. There is wonderful joy ahead, even though you must endure many trials for a little while. These trials will show that your faith is genuine. It is being tested as fire tests and purifies gold—though your faith is far more precious than mere gold. So when your faith remains strong through many trials, it will bring you much praise and glory and honor on the day when Jesus Christ is revealed to the whole world." What are some of the ways your faith has been tested? What trials have you faced?

think on it

What have you learned from these "fires"—these battles? How have you grown stronger as a result?

Where is your faith being challenged now? What do you need to believe God for?

In Luke 18:27, Jesus said, "What is impossible for people is possible with God." Other versions (and other verses) say, "With God all things are possible" (Matthew 19:26 AMP). Or "All things are possible for the one who believes and trusts [in Me]!" (Mark 9:23 AMP). How do these words speak to your heart today?

Act on It

Ephesians 6:10–11 says, "Be strong in the Lord and in His mighty power. Put on all of God's armor so that you will be able to stand firm against all strategies of the devil." (The Enemy wants to distract us from fulfilling God's plans and purpose for us, filling our hearts and minds with doubt and fear.)

The armor God has given us to protect us includes "the shield of faith." Design your own shield of faith below. Decorate it with images, words, or scriptures that affirm, express, or build up your faith.

HOLD UP THE SHIELD OF FAITH TO STOP THE FIERY ARROWS OF THE DEVIL.

EPHESIANS 6:16

Day
8

Rise Up *in* Love

Each day the Lord *pours his unfailing love upon me, and through each night I sing his songs, praying to God who gives me life.*

PSALM 42:8

For this is how God loved the world: He gave his one and only Son, so that everyone who believes in him will not perish but have eternal life.

JOHN 3:16

Ephesians 2:4–5

God is so rich in mercy, and he loved us so much, that even though we were dead because of our sins, he gave us life when he raised Christ from the dead.

Romans 8:31–39

If God is for us, who can ever be against us? Since he did not spare even his own Son but gave him up for us all, won't he also give us everything else? Who dares accuse us whom God has chosen for his own? No one—for God himself has given us right standing with himself. Who then will condemn us? No one—for Christ Jesus died for us and was raised to life for us, and he is sitting in the place of honor at God's right hand, pleading for us. Can anything ever separate us from Christ's love? Does it mean he no longer loves us if we have trouble or calamity, or are persecuted, or hungry, or destitute, or in danger, or threatened with death? . . . No, despite all these things, overwhelming victory is ours through Christ, who loved us. And I am convinced that nothing can ever separate us from God's love. Neither death nor life, neither angels nor demons, neither our fears for today nor our worries about tomorrow—not even the powers of hell can separate us from God's love. No power in the sky above or in the earth below—indeed, nothing in all creation will ever be able to separate us from the love of God that is revealed in Christ Jesus our Lord.

A NOTE FROM *Candace*

Rise Up in Love

This is the good news, friends. The *best* news. Ever.

Nothing can ever separate us from God's love.

Not our brokenness, not our weakness, not our failures or mistakes.

Not our troubles or trials.

Not our worries, doubts, or fears.

Not our confusion, not distractions.

Not our questions.

Nothing in all creation. *All* of it!

God's love is so high, so long, so deep, and so wide that we can never get to the end of it!

We can hardly wrap our minds around it.

We will spend a lifetime learning to receive it.

Learning to live in it.

Learning to grow in it.

Learning to show it and share it with others.

Even then, the adventure will have just begun. We will have all eternity—forever and ever and ever—for more of the same!

It's a never-ending love story.

Each page, each chapter, better than the last. Richer, deeper, more layered and complex.

And yet incredibly simple.

He loves us.

It's His love that lifts us up.

It's in His love that we rise up.

Redeemed, restored, healed, forgiven.

Full of life, full of hope, full of peace, full of joy.

Full of love for Him.

think on it

When did your love story with Jesus begin? When were you first aware of His love for you----and yours for Him?

What does His love mean to you?

think on it

How has your love for God grown? How has it been stretched or deepened? What are you learning about His love for you and your love for Him?

How does He show His love for you? How do you show your love for Him?

Act on It

You don't ever have to play "He Loves Me, He Loves Me Not" with Jesus. The answer is always the same: He loves you *always*! Fully and completely. Absolutely unconditionally. And His love for you will never change.

Look up Psalm 136:1 in the New International Version and write it below.

Now take a few moments to celebrate this glorious truth today! If you can, pick (or purchase) some daisies and put them in a place where you will see them often and be reminded of God's enduring and unfailing love for you! Imagine "He loves me" written on each of the petals (yes, over and over and over again). Take it to heart.

I WILL BE GLAD AND REJOICE IN YOUR UNFAILING LOVE.

PSALM 31:7

Day 9

Rise Up *in* Purpose

And we know [with great confidence] that God [who is deeply concerned about us] causes all things to work together [as a plan] for good for those who love God, to those who are called according to His plan and purpose.

ROMANS 8:28 AMP

For we are His workmanship [His own master work, a work of art], created in Christ Jesus [reborn from above—spiritually transformed, renewed, ready to be used] for good works, which God prepared [for us] beforehand [taking paths which He set], so that we would walk in them [living the good life which He prearranged and made ready for us].

EPHESIANS 2:10 AMP

Ephesians 1:11–12
THE MESSAGE

It's in Christ that we find out who we are and what we are living for. Long before we first heard of Christ and got our hopes up, he had his eye on us, had designs on us for glorious living, part of the overall purpose he is working out in everything and everyone.

Psalm 40:5

O LORD my God, you have performed many wonders for us. Your plans for us are too numerous to list. You have no equal. If I tried to recite all your wonderful deeds, I would never come to the end of them.

Psalm 139:16

You saw me before I was born. Every day of my life was recorded in your book. Every moment was laid out before a single day had passed.

Psalm 139:13, 15
THE MESSAGE

Oh yes, you shaped me first inside, then out; you formed me in my mother's womb. . . . You know me inside and out. . . . You know exactly how I was made, bit by bit, how I was sculpted from nothing into something.

Psalm 139:14
NIV

I praise you because I am fearfully and wonderfully made; your works are wonderful, I know that full well.

Psalm 138:8

The LORD will work out His plans for my life—for your faithful love, O LORD, endures forever.

Rise Up in Purpose

"'For I know the plans I have for you,' declares the LORD, 'plans to prosper you and not to harm you, plans to give you hope and a future'" (Jeremiah 29:11 NIV).

I love knowing that God has a plan. Don't you? He created us for a reason—in this time, in this place, in this season. Not only that—He has a purpose for us that extends beyond this life and into eternity.

He wants us to join Him in His work. He has good things for us to do!

And nothing can mess up His plan—not me, not you.

In the Bible, God once told the prophet Jeremiah to go and visit a pottery. As Jeremiah watched the potter at the wheel, he noticed something: "Whenever the pot the potter was working on turned out badly, as sometimes happens when you are working with clay, the potter would simply start over and use the same clay to make another pot" (Jeremiah 18:4 THE MESSAGE).

God said to Jeremiah, "Did you see that? Did you get it? I can do the very same thing with you!"

Isn't that a relief?

Our failures and mistakes aren't the end of the world.

Our brokenness doesn't get the final word.

Isn't that amazing?

God is infinitely patient and incredibly skilled at His work. He will make and remake us as many times as it takes.

He will keep working on us. Keep working in us. Keep working all things together for our good.

In Philippians 1:6, Paul said this: "I am confident that the Creator, who has begun such a great work among you, *will not stop in mid-design but will* keep perfecting you until the day Jesus the Anointed, *our Liberating King, returns to redeem the world*" (THE VOICE).

That's good news too!

think on it

What does it mean to you to know that God not only has a wonderful master plan—a grand purpose and design for all of us (together)—but that He also has a plan and a purpose specifically for you? How does this motivate, encourage, or inspire you?

The Bible tells us there's even a purpose for our weakness: "We have this *precious* treasure [the good news about salvation] in [unworthy] earthen vessels [of human frailty], so that the grandeur *and* surpassing greatness of the power will be [shown to be] from God [His sufficiency] and not from ourselves" (2 Corinthians 4:7 AMP). How does this thought motivate, encourage, or inspire you?

think on it

In 2 Timothy 3:16–17, it says, "Every part of Scripture is God-breathed and useful one way or another—showing us truth, exposing our rebellion, correcting our mistakes, training us to live God's way. Through the Word we are put together and shaped up for the tasks God has for us" (THE MESSAGE). How is God's Word helping shape you? What are you learning? Which verses are really speaking to you right now?

Act on It

Draw a pot below. Add color or pattern as you reflect on what it means to be God's masterpiece—His work of art—designed for a purpose, created to do good things that He planned for you long ago (Ephesians 2:10). Bonus points if you can pull out and use a ceramic mug or vase as a little reminder of this truth—or sign up for a pottery class or visit a pottery studio sometime this week!

O LORD, YOU ARE OUR FATHER. WE ARE THE CLAY, AND YOU ARE THE POTTER. WE ALL ARE FORMED BY YOUR HAND.

ISAIAH 64:8

Day
10

Rise Up *in* Passion

Love the Lord God with all your passion and prayer and intelligence and energy.

MARK 12:30 THE MESSAGE

Make a careful exploration of who you are and the work you have been given, and then sink yourself into that. Don't be impressed with yourself. Don't compare yourself with others. Each of you must take responsibility for doing the creative best you can with your own life.

GALATIANS 6:4 THE MESSAGE

Colossians 3:23–24

Work willingly at whatever you do, as though you were working for the Lord rather than for people. Remember that the Lord will give you an inheritance as your reward, and that the Master you are serving is Christ.

Ephesians 6:6–8
THE MESSAGE

Don't just do what you have to do to get by, but work heartily, as Christ's servants doing what God wants you to do. And work with a smile on your face, always keeping in mind that no matter who happens to be giving the orders, you're really serving God.

Romans 12:11
THE MESSAGE

Don't burn out; keep yourselves fueled and aflame. Be alert servants of the Master, cheerfully expectant.

Titus 2:13–14
THE VOICE

Watch for His return; expect the blessed hope *we all will share* when our great God and Savior, Jesus the Anointed, appears again. . . . He will also prepare a community . . . that He would call His own—people who are passionate about doing the right thing.

1 Corinthians 15:58
THE MESSAGE

With all this going for us, my dear, dear friends, stand your ground. And don't hold back. Throw yourselves into the work of the Master, confident that nothing you do for him is a waste of time or effort.

Proverbs 16:3
AMP

Commit your works to the LORD [submit and trust them to Him], and your plans will succeed [if you respond to His will and guidance].

A NOTE FROM Candace

Rise Up in Passion

Answering God's call to rise and renew means living with purpose and with passion! No sleepwalking through this amazing life He's given us!

No half-hearted effort, going through the motions, just passing the time.

No phoning it in, failing to show up with our game face on.

The stakes are too high. And the rewards too great to be missed.

The Bible talks a lot about being eager to do what God has called us to do—not reluctant, certainly not resigned or resentful.

Not even *just* being willing. No, He wants us to be eager, enthusiastic, passionate.

Whatever we do, God says to do our very best—to do it for Him and for His glory.

Let others see Him shining through us, giving us the skill, the strength, the focus, the motivation, the determination, the grace under pressure.

And He brings the victory!

Because whenever we answer His call, whenever we show up and we love, give, and serve—eagerly, enthusiastically, passionately—we win!

Even when it's not easy. Maybe especially when it's not easy.

Even when we'd rather be doing other things.

Even when we don't get the applause we expected or the appreciation we deserve.

We can find joy, knowing that when our heart's desire is to honor Him—when we're doing what we're doing in obedience to Him, because we love Him and want to serve Him—Jesus sees. He knows. He's proud of us. He applauds, and He approves.

If you think about it, everything He has ever done for us, He did not just willingly but eagerly, enthusiastically, wholeheartedly, passionately.

He was—and is—absolutely committed to us.

A hundred percent.

All in.

By His grace, in His strength, for His glory, we can do the same. We can be the same for Him.

think on it

What are some of the gifts and talents God has given you? What are your strengths?

What skills have you learned? What experience have you gained? What wisdom?

What are your God-given passions—what you *love* to do? What things seem to come naturally (maybe supernaturally!) to you?

think on it

Where do your gifts and passions intersect? In other words, what are you gifted at and love doing so much that it (almost or sometimes) doesn't feel like work? What's something you find great satisfaction in or look forward to?

Where do you currently have the opportunity to serve God and others in this way? How often? If you don't currently serve in this area, what steps can you take to make this a bigger part of your life, your work, your ministry? And how can you serve God passionately where He has you right now?

Act on It

Galatians 4:18 says, "It is a good thing to be passionate in doing good" (THE MESSAGE). And 2 Timothy 2:22 encourages, "*Direct your passion to* chasing after righteousness, faithfulness, love, and peace" (THE VOICE).

I'm sure you've heard of a mission statement or purpose statement or vision statement. It's a way to communicate—to yourself and to others—what you're all about. It's a way to direct your passion—to think through and stay focused on what really matters to you—especially when you feel pulled in so many different directions.

Today, try writing a passion statement. See if you can answer these questions in your statement:

- What am I truly passionate about?
- What do I believe with all my heart about who God is and who He created me to be?
- What do I believe about God's calling on my life—His plans and purposes for me?
- What role do I have the privilege of playing in this purpose? How can I be responsible with it?
- What are my life goals? My hopes? My dreams?
- What will I do to make these things a reality?

COMMIT EVERYTHING YOU DO TO THE LORD.

TRUST HIM, AND HE WILL HELP YOU.

PSALM 37:5

Day

11

Rise Up *in* Wisdom

Joyful is the person who finds wisdom, the one who gains understanding.

PROVERBS 3:13

We have not stopped praying for you since we first heard about you. We ask God to give you complete knowledge of his will and to give you spiritual wisdom and understanding. Then the way you live will always honor and please the Lord, and your lives will produce every kind of good fruit. All the while, you will grow as you learn to know God better and better.

COLOSSIANS 1:9–10

Colossians 2:3
AMP

In whom are hidden all the treasures of wisdom and knowledge [regarding the word and purposes of God].

Ephesians 1:6, 8

So we praise God for the glorious grace he has poured out on us who belong to his dear Son. . . . He has showered his kindness on us, along with all wisdom and understanding.

Romans 11:33–36
THE MESSAGE

Have you ever come on anything quite like this extravagant generosity of God, this deep, deep wisdom? It's way over our heads. We'll never figure it out. Is there anyone around who can explain God? Anyone smart enough to tell him what to do? Anyone who has done him such a huge favor that God has to ask his advice? Everything comes from him; everything happens through him; everything ends up in him. Always glory! Always praise! Yes. Yes. Yes.

James 1:5
TLB

If you want to know what God wants you to do, ask him, and he will gladly tell you, for he is always ready to give a bountiful supply of wisdom to all who ask him; he will not resent it.

James 3:17

The wisdom from above is first of all pure. It is also peace loving, gentle at all times, and willing to yield to others. It is full of mercy and the fruit of good deeds.

Rise Up in Wisdom

I'm so thankful I don't have to have all the answers. I don't have to figure out this life all on my own. I don't have to depend on my own wisdom, my own knowledge and understanding.

I have the Spirit of God living in me.

I have the wisdom of God, the Word of God, to guide me.

I can ask the Creator of the universe—the One who created me—because He always knows what is best for me.

He tells me to come to Him anytime, anyplace, and ask Him anything!

I can ask Him what to do (or not do), what to say (or not say) in any given situation.

I can ask Him how to live my life, how to love my family and friends, how to carry out my responsibilities and make the most of all the opportunities He's given me.

Lately, He's been showing me how to grow (a little) older gracefully! How to accept my limitations and temper my expectations. How to make peace with my body.

Really, I'm learning how to treat all of me—body, mind, soul, and spirit—more gently, compassionately, lovingly, and gratefully. And to treat others the same way.

It's been eye-opening to realize how hard I've pushed myself, how fearless—maybe a bit careless—I used to be, how crazy some of my expectations were . . . all that pressure I put on myself to accomplish and achieve.

These days, I'm asking Him to show me what He has for me—what His plans and purposes are.

I'm asking Him to help me rise up and be the woman He wants me to be.

I'm asking Him for wisdom to know what He wants me to do, where He wants me to go, what He wants me to see. I'm asking Him to show me His priorities.

With the psalmist, I pray, "Lead me by your truth and teach me, for you are the God who saves me" (Psalm 25:5).

I know He will give me everything I need day by day—including the wisdom to walk in His ways.

think on it

Proverbs 3:5–6 says, "Trust God from the bottom of your heart; don't try to figure out everything on your own. Listen for God's voice in everything you do, everywhere you go; he's the one who will keep you on track" (THE MESSAGE). How do you listen for His voice? How do you know when He's speaking to you?

Where—specifically—do you need God's wisdom and guidance today?

think on it

If you could go back in time and share some words of wisdom with your younger self, what would they be? What are some of the most important things you've learned in your life to date? How did you learn these things? How do they help you today?

Proverbs 4:5 says, "*Whatever it takes to* gain Wisdom, *do it*. To gain understanding, *do it!*" (THE VOICE). What are you doing to continue to learn and grow, to gain wisdom and understanding in your life now?

Act on It

In the book of Proverbs, wisdom is personified as a woman, "Lady Wisdom," calling out to everyone who will hear, urging them to listen to her voice and learn from her. Further on in Proverbs 31, we're given a description of the "Virtuous Woman"—a kind of role model, an ideal—and it says, "She speaks with wisdom" (v. 26 NIV).

How do you picture Lady Wisdom? What image comes to mind when you think of a "wise woman"? Draw a picture below or look for one online that you can print and paste here. Maybe it's someone you know. Maybe—by God's grace and in His strength—it is someone you see in the mirror.

COME AND LISTEN TO MY COUNSEL. I'LL SHARE MY HEART WITH YOU AND MAKE YOU WISE.

PROVERBS 1:23

Day
12

Rise Up *in* Worship

Worship God if you want the best; worship opens doors to all his goodness.

PSALM 34:9 THE MESSAGE

Speak to one another with the words of psalms, hymns, and sacred songs; sing hymns and psalms to the Lord with praise in your hearts.

EPHESIANS 5:19 GNT

2 Corinthians 4:13–14
THE MESSAGE

Just like the psalmist who wrote, "I believed it, so I said it," we say what we believe. And what we believe is that the One who raised up the Master Jesus will just as certainly raise us up.

Romans 16:25
THE MESSAGE

All of our praise rises to the One who is strong enough to make *you* strong.

Psalm 27:4–6

The one thing I ask of the LORD—the thing I seek most—is to live in the house of the LORD all the days of my life, delighting in the LORD's perfections and meditating in his Temple. For he will conceal me there when troubles come; he will hide me in his sanctuary. He will place me out of reach on a high rock. Then I will hold my head high above my enemies who surround me. At his sanctuary I will offer sacrifices with shouts of joy, singing and praising the LORD with music.

Psalm 21:13

Rise up, O LORD, in all your power. With music and singing we celebrate your mighty acts.

Psalm 5:11

Let all who take refuge in you rejoice; let them sing joyful praises forever. Spread your protection over them, that all who love your name may be filled with joy.

Psalm 89:15

Happy are those who hear the joyful call to worship, for they will walk in the light of your presence, LORD.

A NOTE FROM *Candace*

Rise Up in Worship

Not long ago, I was reminded in a very real way just how vital it is to rise up in worship—just how powerful praising God can be.

My family had come under attack, but I didn't realize it at first. I didn't see what was happening to us right away.

Our house is usually a pretty peaceful and happy place. But all of a sudden it seemed we were all irritable and on edge. We were going at each other, reacting in anger and frustration over the silliest things. This went on for several days. Our brokenness was front and center!

Ephesians 5:14 says, "The light makes everything visible. . . . 'Awake, O sleeper, rise up . . . and Christ will give you light.'"

Thankfully, that's what happened. Jesus gave me a lightbulb moment.

I realized we were in a battle, but not with each other.

As it says in Ephesians 6:12, "We are not fighting against flesh-and-blood enemies, but against evil rulers and authorities of the unseen world, against mighty powers in this dark world, and against evil spirits in the heavenly places."

In our family, we were fighting a spirit of irritability, a spirit of crankiness, a spirit of confusion, sent by the Enemy of our souls.

We forget sometimes that this Enemy is very real—that he's hell-bent on attacking us every single day of our lives. The Bible says he's "like a roaring lion," and he's always looking for ways to devour us (1 Peter 5:8).

But thanks to Jesus, this Enemy has no authority.

We don't belong to the Enemy. We're not under his control.

We belong to Jesus.

Jesus has all authority, all power. He reigns in my home and in yours.

So as soon as it hit me what was going on, I called on the Holy Spirit to help us. I prayed against any evil spirit in our house. And I got my praise on—I put on my worship music and played it all the time, flooding our home with words of Scripture, words of truth, words of hope and healing and courage and wisdom and power.

God's Word. God's truth. God's power.

And that made all the difference.

Take a few moments to pray over your home, your family, your heart—and ask Jesus to shine a light on any areas that are under attack. Ask Him to show you where the battle is taking place, and jot down anything specific that comes to mind.

Colossians 1:12–14 says that God has made it possible for us to "share in the inheritance that belongs to his people, who live in the light. For he has rescued us from the kingdom of darkness and transferred us into the Kingdom of his dear Son, who purchased our freedom and forgave our sins." Thank God for rescuing you and your loved ones. Pray for any friends or family who have yet to be "rescued." Write specific names in the space provided and draw a circle or a heart around them to represent being surrounded by God's loving care, safe in His love.

think on it

In light of what God has done for us, Hebrews 13:15 says, "Let us offer through Jesus a continual sacrifice of praise to God, proclaiming our allegiance to his name." Go ahead and proclaim your allegiance—declare His authority in your heart and your home. Maybe include or end with the words of Joshua 24:15: "As for me and my family, we will serve the LORD."

In John 4:23–24, *The Message* explains, "That's the kind of people the Father is out looking for: those who are simply and honestly *themselves* before him in their worship. . . . Those who worship him must do it out of their very being, their spirits, their true selves, in adoration." What does this mean to you? What does it—or might it—look like in your life?

Act on It

Colossians 3:16 says, "Let the message about Christ, in all its richness, fill your lives. Teach and counsel each other with all the wisdom he gives. Sing psalms and hymns and spiritual songs to God with thankful hearts."

It's time, friend. Don't sit there a minute longer—get your praise on! Rise up and worship! Do it in whatever way feels authentic to you. You can sing or shout, clap your hands, or dance. Play a beloved hymn or praise chorus, or make up one of your own and write it below.

To keep the worship rising, make a playlist of your favorites—hymns, contemporary choruses, gospel anthems—and play them wherever you can, as often as you can. Text a link to a video or the lyrics of one of the songs to your friends and family—or post them on social media. And ask your friends and family to share their favorites with you.

THE LORD IS MY STRENGTH AND MY SONG; HE HAS GIVEN ME VICTORY.

EXODUS 15:2

Day
13

Rise Up *in* Grace

"My grace is sufficient for you [My lovingkindness and My mercy are more than enough—always available—regardless of the situation]; for [My] power is being perfected [and is completed and shows itself most effectively] in [your] weakness."

2 CORINTHIANS 12:9 AMP

All praise to God, the Father of our Lord Jesus Christ, who has blessed us with every spiritual blessing in the heavenly realms because we are united with Christ. Even before he made the world, God loved us and chose us in Christ to be holy and without fault in his eyes. God decided in advance to adopt us into his own family by bringing us to himself through Jesus Christ. This is what he wanted to do, and it gave him great pleasure. So we praise God for the glorious grace he has poured out on us who belong to his dear Son. He is so rich in kindness and grace that he purchased our freedom with the blood of his Son and forgave our sins.

EPHESIANS 1:3–7

Ephesians 2:7–8
THE MESSAGE

Now God has us where he wants us, with all the time in this world and the next to shower grace and kindness upon us in Christ Jesus. Saving is all his idea, and all his work. All we do is trust him enough to let him do it. It's God's gift from start to finish!

Colossians 1:6

This same Good News that came to you is going out all over the world. It is bearing fruit everywhere by changing lives, just as it changed your lives from the day you first heard and understood the truth about God's wonderful grace.

2 Corinthians 8:9
AMP

For you are recognizing [more clearly] the grace of our Lord Jesus Christ [His astonishing kindness, His generosity, His gracious favor], that though He was rich, yet for your sake He became poor, so that by His poverty you might become rich (abundantly blessed).

James 4:6
AMP

He gives us more and more grace [through the power of the Holy Spirit to defy sin and live an obedient life that reflects both our faith and our gratitude for our salvation].

Rise Up in Grace

God's grace is so much greater—greater than our sin. Greater than the most messed-up, mixed-up part of us. Greater than our brokenness, guilt, and shame.

It's His grace that gives us strength to rise up each new day.

Rise up and renew.

We don't have to live up to an impossible standard of perfection—impossible for us, anyway.

Grace has us covered.

We don't have to live with unrealistic expectations of what we should look like, what we should *be* like, what we should do or say.

Grace has us covered.

Make a mistake and it seems like the world won't let you forget it. God says, "What mistake? I really don't remember" (Hebrews 8:12, my paraphrase).

Because grace.

God says not to worry about our weakness. Not to obsess over our flaws or our failures.

Because grace.

"My grace is all you need. My power works best in weakness" (2 Corinthians 12:9).

It's in our weakness that His power shines brightest. That's when He does what only He can do—what He does best:

He makes something beautiful out of this hot mess (Ecclesiastes 3:11).

So we can bound out of bed with a smile on our face.

We can take heart and take on the world.

We can live well and love well—and bear with others in their weakness too.

Because grace.

think on it

How has God shown His grace to you?

How would you describe grace? What does grace look like? What does it feel like?

How have others shown you grace?

think on it

Who is God calling you to show grace to?

What can you do to show that person (or people) grace?

Act on It

John 1:16 says that out of God's "fullness [the superabundance of His grace and truth] we have all received grace upon grace [spiritual blessing upon spiritual blessing, favor upon favor, and gift heaped upon gift]" (AMP).

Sometimes we forget just how rich God's grace is—and how blessed we are. So in the words of an old hymn, let's "count our blessings" today! Write down as many gifts of grace—as many blessings God has given you—as you can think of in three minutes.

MAY GOD GIVE YOU MORE AND MORE GRACE AND PEACE AS YOU GROW IN YOUR KNOWLEDGE OF GOD AND JESUS OUR LORD.

2 PETER 1:2

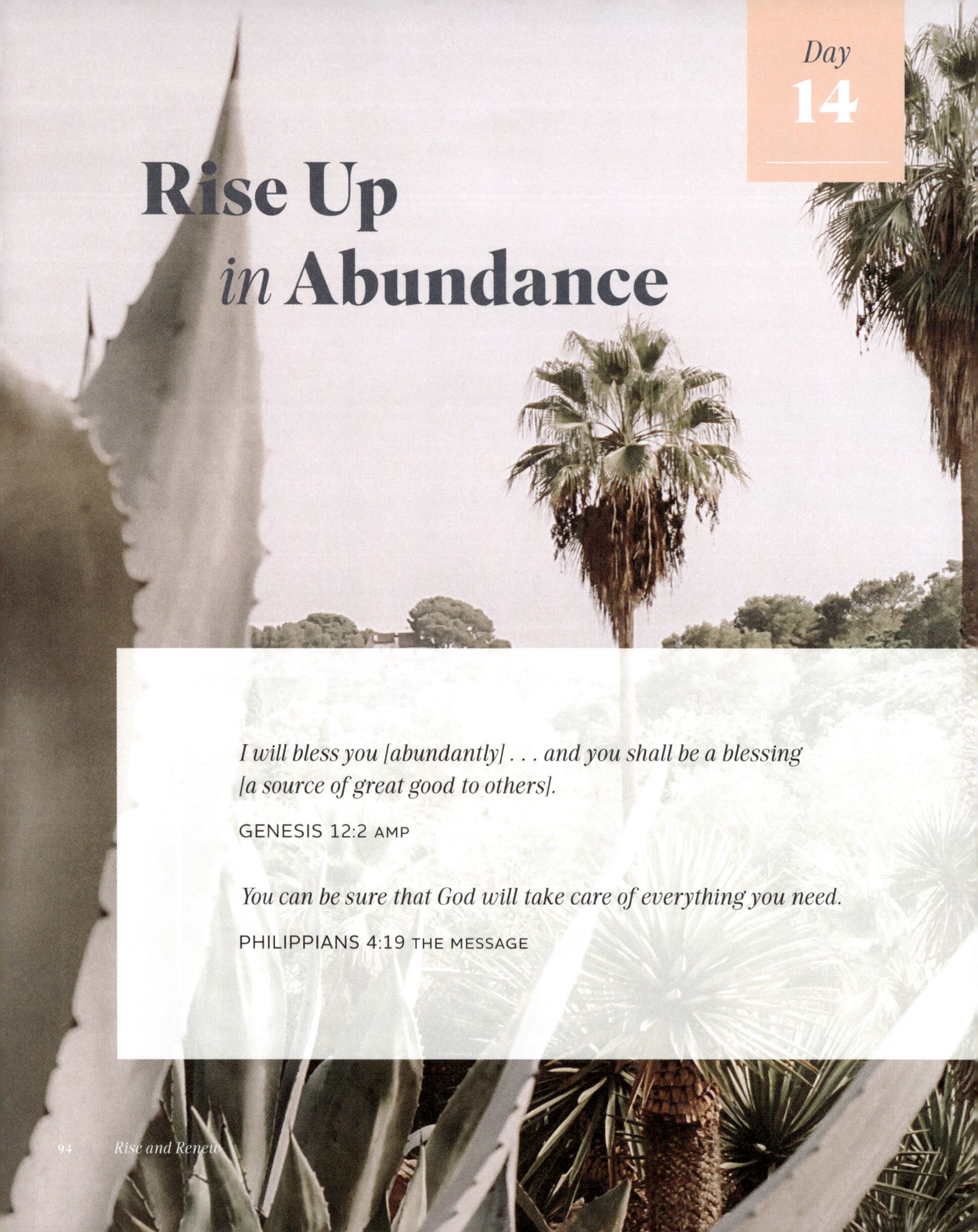

Day
14

Rise Up *in* Abundance

I will bless you [abundantly] . . . and you shall be a blessing [a source of great good to others].

GENESIS 12:2 AMP

You can be sure that God will take care of everything you need.

PHILIPPIANS 4:19 THE MESSAGE

2 Peter 1:3 THE MESSAGE	Everything that goes into a life of pleasing God has been miraculously given to us by getting to know, personally and intimately, the One who invited us to God. The best invitation we ever received!
Ephesians 1:9 THE MESSAGE	*Abundantly* free! He thought of everything, provided for everything we could possibly need.
John 1:16 THE MESSAGE	We all live off his generous abundance, gift after gift after gift.
2 Corinthians 9:8	God will generously provide all you need. Then you will always have everything you need and plenty left over to share with others.
Acts 20:35	Remember the words of the Lord Jesus: "It is more blessed to give than to receive."
Matthew 10:8	Give as freely as you have received!
Luke 6:38 THE MESSAGE	Give away your life; you'll find life given back, but not merely given back—given back with bonus and blessing.
2 Corinthians 9:8 THE MESSAGE	God can pour on the blessings in astonishing ways so that you're ready for anything and everything.

A NOTE FROM *Candace*

Rise Up in Abundance

God doesn't do anything halfway. Or half-heartedly. No, He goes all the way, above and beyond, over the top. He gives generously, *abundantly.* So much more than enough. Until we're full to overflowing.

Now, the gift doesn't always come into our lives the way that we expect or imagine. Or on our timetable. But it's there. *He* is there. In His love for us, He always shows up. He always prepares and provides everything we need, in every way—physically, mentally, emotionally, and spiritually—even if it's in a way that's different from what we expected or hoped.

We can rise up and stand tall, heads held high, knowing that our Father is the King of kings.

His resources are absolutely unlimited! As the Bible puts it, He owns "the cattle on a thousand hills" (Psalm 50:10). He owns everything—the earth and everyone and everything in it. It belongs to Him.

And His generosity never runs out. God gives freely to us, again and again.

Now, it's not that He doesn't ever allow us to go through hard times or call us to places of suffering and sacrifice. In fact, Jesus said, "Here on earth you will have many trials and sorrows" (John 16:33).

But you know that verse in Philippians? "I can do all things through Christ who strengthens me" (4:13 NKJV). That's what this verse is really talking about.

The Amplified Bible puts it this way:

> I know how to get along and live humbly [in difficult times], and I also know how to enjoy abundance *and* live in prosperity. In any and every circumstance I have learned the secret [of facing life], whether well-fed or going hungry, whether having an abundance or being in need. I can do all things [which He has called me to do] through Him who strengthens *and* empowers me [to fulfill His purpose—I am self-sufficient in Christ's sufficiency; I am ready for anything and equal to anything through Him who infuses me with inner strength and confident peace]. (Philippians 4:12–13)

Hallelujah! Praise God! We have the Spirit of God, the Spirit of Jesus, living in us and through us—and He is more than enough. He is all we need.

think on it

What are some of the ways God has provided for you in the past? Think of physical, mental, emotional, and spiritual provisions.

What do you need today? Think of physical, mental, emotional, and spiritual needs.

Ask God right now to provide for each and every one of these needs.

Consider closing your prayer with the words Paul used in Ephesians 3:20–21: "Now to Him who is able to [carry out His purpose and] do superabundantly more than all that we dare ask or think [infinitely beyond our greatest prayers, hopes, or dreams], according to His power that is at work within us, to Him be the glory in the church and in Christ Jesus throughout all generations forever and ever. Amen" (AMP).

Act on It

The Bible tells us that our generosity to others springs from our gratitude to God for His generosity to us—and from the security that we have in Christ. We're free to give because we know we don't have to hoard or hang on to anything. God has been providing for us *abundantly*, and He will keep providing for us *abundantly*. And through us, He will provide *abundantly* for others.

Take a few minutes to list below five things you're thankful for—gifts, resources, or things that you've been blessed with or given.

Now list five things you have available to give—gifts, resources, or things you can bless others with. Include specific ways you can share these things this week.

THE ONE WHO BLESSES OTHERS IS ABUNDANTLY BLESSED; THOSE WHO HELP OTHERS ARE HELPED.

PROVERBS 11:25 THE MESSAGE

Day
15

Rise Up *in* Life

Do your very best to be found living at your best.

2 PETER 3:14 THE MESSAGE

Everything that we have—right thinking and right living, a clean slate and a fresh start—comes from God by way of Jesus Christ.

1 CORINTHIANS 1:30 THE MESSAGE

John 1:4
THE MESSAGE

Everything was created through him; nothing—not one thing!—came into being without him. What came into existence was Life, and the Life was Light to live by.

1 John 4:13
THE MESSAGE

This is how we know we're living steadily and deeply in him, and he in us: He's given us life from his life, from his very own Spirit.

Colossians 3:4
THE MESSAGE

Your old life is dead. Your new life, which is your *real* life—even though invisible to spectators—is with Christ in God. *He* is your life.

1 John 5:11–12

This is what God has testified: He has given us eternal life, and this life is in his Son. Whoever has the Son has life.

Ephesians 3:14–19
THE MESSAGE

My response is to get down on my knees before the Father, this magnificent Father who parcels out all heaven and earth. I ask him to strengthen you by his Spirit . . . that Christ will live in you as you open the door and invite him in. And I ask him that with both feet planted firmly on love, you'll be able to take in with all followers of Jesus the extravagant dimensions of Christ's love. Reach out and experience the breadth! Test its length! Plumb the depths! Rise to the heights! Live full lives, full in the fullness of God.

A NOTE FROM *Candace*

Rise Up in Life

We call her "the woman at the well" because we don't know her name. But Jesus did. And John 4 tells us that after she met Jesus, she was never the same.

She'd spent her entire life looking for love in all the wrong places, trying to find it in one failed relationship after another, so many that it was a scandal. Everyone knew her story—or thought they knew—and gossiped about it.

She was desperate for a sense of purpose, something to give her life meaning. But nothing—and no one—could satisfy the deep hunger inside. Nothing and no one had ever been able to quench her thirst.

No one but Jesus.

When He met her at the well, He asked her for a drink and then offered her something so much more: living water.

"Those who drink the water I give will never be thirsty again," He explained. "It becomes a fresh, bubbling spring within them, giving them eternal life" (v. 14).

He gives us His life—His Spirit—to live in us, to fill all our empty places, to fill our hunger, and to quench our thirst.

His life strengthens us, energizes us, empowers us to live life more fully than we could ever have imagined.

In John 10:10, He calls it a rich and satisfying life—a better life—an abundant life (ESV) that is full to overflowing!

This life is nothing we earn—nothing we work for or strive for or somehow prove ourselves worthy or deserving of. We couldn't earn it, even if we tried!

"When you open your hand, you satisfy the hunger and thirst of every living thing" (Psalm 145:16).

It's a gift.

So what we do is receive it. Open it up, so to speak—explore it, embrace it—with an open mind, open heart, and willing spirit.

Rise up and learn how to live an abundant life!

think on it

What have you been "hungry" or "thirsty" for?

What empty spaces have you tried to fill in your heart? How did you try to fill them? With what? How has that worked for you?

How is the "living water"—the life that Jesus freely gives—different from what the world tries to sell us?

think on it

How does Jesus satisfy you? How does He quench your thirst? In what ways do you experience His life flowing in and through you?

In Psalm 42:8, the psalmist exclaimed, "Each day the Lord pours his unfailing love upon me, and through each night I sing his songs, praying to God who gives me life." Take a few moments now to express your love and gratitude to Him for all that He's done for you.

Act on It

In John 7:38, Jesus said, "If you believe in Me . . . rivers of living water will flow from within you" (THE VOICE). Other verses—and other translations—use words like "streams" or "fountains" or "oceans" or "wellsprings" to describe the vibrant, creative, refreshing life of Christ that flows in us and through us.

Draw a picture (or find one that you can print and cut and paste) in the space below that represents what you imagine when you think about "living water"—what this life in Christ looks like and feels like to you.

GOD—YOU'RE MY GOD! I CAN'T GET ENOUGH OF YOU! . . . SO HERE I AM IN THE PLACE OF WORSHIP, EYES OPEN, DRINKING IN YOUR STRENGTH AND GLORY. IN YOUR GENEROUS LOVE I AM REALLY LIVING AT LAST!

PSALM 63:1–3 THE MESSAGE

Day

16

Renew *Your* Heart

Let all that I am praise the Lord; *with my whole heart, I will praise his holy name.*

PSALM 103:1

Generous in love—God, give grace! Huge in mercy—wipe out my bad record. Scrub away my guilt, soak out my sins in your laundry. I know how bad I've been; my sins are staring me down. . . . You have all the facts before you; whatever you decide about me is fair. I've been out of step with you for a long time, in the wrong since before I was born. What you're after is truth from the inside out. Enter me, then; conceive a new, true life.

PSALM 51:1–6 THE MESSAGE

Psalm 51:10–12
THE VOICE

Create in me a clean heart, O God; restore within me a sense of being brand new. Do not throw me far away from Your presence, and do not remove Your Holy Spirit from me. Give back to me the *deep* delight of being saved by You; let Your willing Spirit sustain me.

Psalm 51:16–17

You do not desire a sacrifice, or I would offer one. You do not want a burnt offering. The sacrifice you desire is a broken spirit. You will not reject a broken and repentant heart, O God.

Isaiah 1:18
NIV

"Come now, let us settle the matter," says the LORD. "Though your sins are like scarlet, they shall be as white as snow; though they are red as crimson, they shall be like wool."

Ezekiel 36:26

I will give you a new heart, and I will put a new spirit in you. I will take out your stony, stubborn heart and give you a tender, responsive heart.

A NOTE FROM *Candace*

Renew Your Heart

The Bible tells us our hearts have a way of wandering . . . growing stubborn or rebellious or hard.

Like ground in which nothing can grow.

But God, in His mercy, loves us far too much to leave us in that miserable condition.

He has hundreds—thousands—of ways of getting through to us. Plowing up that dry, rocky ground. Pulling the weeds. Planting new seeds. Watering the newly softened soil.

It can be a painful process, especially when we've really let things go.

It's so much easier, so much better, when we continually open our hearts to Him, and invite Him in. When we confess our sin quickly, as soon as we see it, as soon as we sense it. Root it out right away.

Take good care of the new heart, the new love, and the new life He's given us.

Renew it day by day.

We don't have to live with guilt and shame. Ever.

In 1 John 1:9, the Bible reminds us, "If we own up to our sins, God shows that He is faithful and just by forgiving us of our sins and purifying us from the pollution of all the bad things we have done" (THE VOICE).

Immediately. Instantaneously.

The psalmist prayed, "Create in me a clean heart, O God; restore within me a sense of being brand new" (Psalm 51:10 THE VOICE).

And God did.

He does.

He will—today!

think on it

Take a few moments to prayerfully consider the condition of your heart today. Any weeds growing? (Any sin you need to confess?) Any rough patches? (Any hardness of heart, bitterness, or resentment?)

Write out a short prayer, asking God to forgive you right now and to work in your heart today.

The psalmist exclaimed, "With all my heart I will praise you, O Lord my God. I will give glory to your name forever" (Psalm 86:12)! Thank God for what He has done for you, and what—in His love for you—He continues to do.

Psalm 119:34 says, "Give me understanding and I will obey your instructions; I will put them into practice with all my heart." Ask God to show you what you can do to renew your heart, to keep it open and tender and responsive to Him.

What is He calling you to do? What instructions has He given you to "put into practice" today?

Act on It

Many of us spent our teenage years drawing fancy hearts all over the place—on our schoolbooks and in our diaries or journals, in notes to friends, on our arms or our hands. Maybe it's been a while, but I bet you haven't forgotten how, which is good, because it's time to draw those hearts again, this time in the space below—filling each one with a love note to Jesus, a word of thanks or praise! Tell Him how much you love Him, how much He means to you. Ask Him to renew your heart in His love—to keep your heart His—forever and ever.

GOD REMAINS THE STRENGTH OF MY HEART; HE IS MINE FOREVER.

PSALM 73:26

Day 17

Renew *Your* Mind

Those who are dominated by the sinful nature think about sinful things, but those who are controlled by the Holy Spirit think about things that please the Spirit.

ROMANS 8:5

Letting your sinful nature control your mind leads to death. But letting the Spirit control your mind leads to life and peace.

ROMANS 8:6

Romans 8:9

But you are not controlled by your sinful nature. You are controlled by the Spirit if you have the Spirit of God living in you.

2 Timothy 1:7
AMP

[He has given us a spirit] of power and of love and of sound judgment *and* personal discipline [abilities that result in a calm, well-balanced mind and self-control].

1 Peter 1:13

So prepare your minds for action and exercise self-control. Put all your hope in the gracious salvation that will come to you when Jesus Christ is revealed to the world.

Colossians 3:1–2
NIV

Since, then, you have been raised with Christ, set your hearts on things above, where Christ is, seated at the right hand of God. Set your minds on things above, not on earthly things.

Ephesians 4:23–24

Let the Spirit renew your thoughts and attitudes. Put on your new nature, created to be like God—truly righteous and holy.

2 Corinthians 10:5
THE MESSAGE

We use our powerful God-tools for . . . fitting every loose thought and emotion and impulse into the structure of life shaped by Christ.

Philippians 4:7
NIV

And the peace of God, which transcends all understanding, will guard your hearts and your minds in Christ Jesus.

A NOTE FROM *Candace*

Renew Your Mind

I'm learning that so many of the battles I face begin in my mind. That's where the temptation starts.

- The temptation to live in the future—mentally planning and preparing and problem-solving—and then I miss being fully present, right where I am.
- The temptation to let my thoughts wander into daydreaming and fantasy that may not be super healthy or productive.
- The temptation to fixate on little irritations and frustrations. Or to rehearse old grievances, reopen old wounds, and relive pain from the past.

Really, with any wise, disciplined, healthy choice I want to make—eating right, exercising, you name it—there's always the temptation to procrastinate, to rationalize, to make up reasons (excuses!) to *do* what I shouldn't do and *not* do what I should.

The more I let myself think about it, the more I let myself mentally go there, the more likely I am to fall headlong into that mess!

That's why in 2 Corinthians 10:5, the Bible urges us to "take captive every thought to make it obedient to Christ" (NIV).

To me, "taking every thought captive" means paying attention when unhelpful or unhealthy thoughts cross my mind and deliberately choosing to rein them in—choosing to redirect them. Choosing to refocus, to "set my mind on things above"—on good and godly things.

It's not always easy, but the Bible tells us that we can do this because we have the Spirit of God living in us. The Holy Spirit is our Helper, our Counselor, our Comforter, our Strengthener (John 14:26 AMP). He's there to remind us of what is good and right and true.

And there's more good news! In 1 Corinthians 2:16, Paul says that we've actually been given "the mind of Christ [to be guided by His thoughts and purposes]" (AMP).

His thoughts are so much higher, so much wiser, than our own (Isaiah 55:8–9).

He can help us win those daily battles in our hearts *and* in our minds.

In Matthew 22:37, Jesus said, "'You must love the Lord your God with all your heart, all your soul, and all your mind.'" What do you think it means to love God with your mind? What does that look like for you?

When it comes to the battlefield of the mind, what are your biggest enemies? What kind of temptations do you face?

think on it

The Bible tells us we don't have to give in to every tempting thought that crosses our minds. "God is faithful, and he will not let you be tempted beyond your ability, but with the temptation he will also provide the way of escape, that you may be able to endure it" (1 Corinthians 10:13 ESV). Put another way: "No test or temptation that comes your way is beyond the course of what others have had to face. All you need to remember is that God will never let you down; he'll never let you be pushed past your limit; he'll always be there to help you come through it" (THE MESSAGE). How do these verses encourage you?

Can you think of some examples of that "way of escape" that God provides? How can you remember to look for it—and take it?

Act on It

In 2 Corinthians 10:4–5, the Bible reminds us, "The weapons we fight with are not the weapons of the world. On the contrary, they have divine power to demolish strongholds. We demolish arguments and every pretension that sets itself up against the knowledge of God, and we take captive every thought to make it obedient to Christ" (NIV).

Today—empowered by the Holy Spirit—practice taking every thought captive. Like a superhero, imagine rounding up your wayward thoughts, wrapping them up in the "lasso of truth." Jot down some of those thoughts and draw a lasso around them, then write words of Scripture, truth, praise, and thanksgiving all around them.

FILL YOUR MINDS WITH *BEAUTY AND* TRUTH.

PHILIPPIANS 4:8 THE VOICE

Day 18

Renew *Your* Strength

I love you, Lord; you are my strength.

PSALM 18:1

May our Lord Jesus Christ himself and God our Father, who loved us and by his grace gave us eternal comfort and a wonderful hope, comfort you and strengthen you in every good thing you do and say.

2 THESSALONIANS 2:16–17

Isaiah 40:28–31

The LORD is the everlasting God, the Creator of all the earth. He never grows weak or weary. No one can measure the depths of his understanding. He gives power to the weak and strength to the powerless. Even youths will become weak and tired, and young men will fall in exhaustion. But those who trust in the LORD will find new strength. They will soar high on wings like eagles. They will run and not grow weary. They will walk and not faint.

Colossians 1:10–12
THE MESSAGE

Be assured that from the first day we heard of you, we haven't stopped praying for you, asking God to give you wise minds and spirits attuned to his will, and so acquire a thorough understanding of the ways in which God works. We pray that you'll live well for the Master, making him proud of you as you work hard. . . . As you learn more and more how God works, you will learn how to do your work. We pray that you'll have the strength to stick it out over the long haul—not the grim strength of gritting your teeth but the glory-strength God gives. It is strength that endures the unendurable and spills over into joy, thanking the Father who makes us strong enough to take part in everything bright and beautiful that he has for us.

Philippians 4:13
AMP

I can do all things [which He has called me to do] through Him who strengthens and empowers me [to fulfill His purpose—I am self-sufficient in Christ's sufficiency; I am ready for anything and equal to anything through Him who infuses me with inner strength and confident peace.]

A NOTE FROM *Candace*

Renew Your Strength

The older I get, the more I understand the truth in the old cliché "move it or lose it!" Our muscles—physical, mental, and spiritual—need to be used. They need to be maintained. They need to be strengthened and renewed.

Not long ago, I went through a time when I had not been working out consistently, and I knew I needed to. I knew that movement was so good for my body. I knew how much better exercise would make me feel—the physical and mental energy it would give me. The mood boost!

But I was tired. I seemed to be fighting against my own will and desire. I couldn't make myself do it! I just couldn't get motivated. It seemed like a mental and spiritual thing as much as a physical one.

The more the battle dragged on, day after day, the more discouraged and defeated I felt.

So I literally started praying every day, asking God to give me victory—asking God to give me the strength and the motivation I needed, just to put on my workout clothes, pull up the video, and hit Play. I promised I would show up—and I prayed that He would be there too. I asked Him to help me do whatever I could do.

And He did.

He was there for me. He helped me.

He renewed my strength.

One day, I got through the workout—and it felt great!

The next day, I took a walk because I could feel my new resolve slipping away. I wasn't quite back in the groove, at full strength just yet. I knew it would feel really good and right to be surrounded by the beauty of God's creation. I knew it would help get me back on track and keep my eyes on Him.

As I walked, I prayed. I kept giving my weakness and my weariness to God, declaring my hope and my trust in Him.

Deuteronomy 11:22 says, "Show love to the LORD your God by walking in his ways and holding tightly to him." So that's what I did.

And now I can say with the psalmist that God "lifted me out of the pit of despair, out of the mud and the mire. He set my feet on solid ground and steadied me as I walked along" (Psalm 40:2).

I know He can do the same for you.

think on it

Psalm 46:1 says, "God is our refuge and strength, always ready to help in times of trouble." And 2 Thessalonians 3:3 assures us, "The Lord is faithful; he will strengthen you and guard you from the evil one." Where do you feel under attack in your life today?

Where do you feel discouraged or defeated?

Where do you need God's protection, strength, or help?

think on it

How have you experienced His protection, His strength, His help in the past? How has God been there for you?

What is your motivation now? Why do you want to do the things you're struggling to do—the things that might feel difficult or impossible to you?

In Psalm 71:7–8, the psalmist exclaimed, "My life is an example to many, because you have been my strength and protection. That is why I can never stop praising you; I declare your glory all day long." How is your life an example—and who are you setting an example for? How might God be glorified by what you're going through, by your perseverance, through the strength He's giving you?

Act on It

With God, all things are possible—even the things that feel impossible, the things that, humanly speaking, in our own strength, we just can't do (Luke 18:27). God can do it! He can work in and through us to accomplish anything He calls us to do. He promises that He will help us. He will renew our strength with each and every step we take.

So choose one thing you believe God is asking you to do, one step that will move you in the right direction. Write it below. Then set an alarm to remind you—at a specific time and date, or every morning or throughout the day—to ask Him to help you, to fill you with His strength. Cup your hands as you pray, remembering to receive all that He has for you.

THE LORD IS MY STRENGTH AND MY SONG; HE HAS GIVEN ME VICTORY.

PSALM 118:14

Day 19

Renew *Your* Love

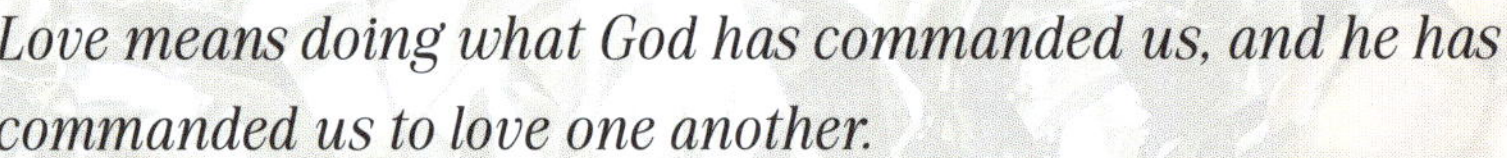

Love means doing what God has commanded us, and he has commanded us to love one another.

2 JOHN 1:6

My beloved friends, let us continue to love each other since love comes from God. Everyone who loves is born of God and experiences a relationship with God. The person who refuses to love doesn't know the first thing about God, because God is love—so you can't know him if you don't love. This is how God showed his love for us: God sent his only Son into the world so we might live through him. This is the kind of love we are talking about—not that we once upon a time loved God, but that he loved us and sent his Son as a sacrifice to clear away our sins and the damage they've done to our relationship with God. My dear, dear friends, if God loved us like this, we certainly ought to love each other. No one has seen God, ever. But if we love one another, God dwells deeply within us, and his love becomes complete in us—perfect love!

1 JOHN 4:7–12 THE MESSAGE

1 Corinthians 13:1–3

If I could speak all the languages of earth and of angels, but didn't love others, I would only be a noisy gong or a clanging cymbal. If I had the gift of prophecy, and if I understood all of God's secret plans and possessed all knowledge, and if I had such faith that I could move mountains, but didn't love others, I would be nothing. If I gave everything I have to the poor and even sacrificed my body, I could boast about it; but if I didn't love others, I would have gained nothing.

1 Corinthians 13:4–7
THE VOICE

Love is patient; love is kind. Love isn't envious, doesn't boast, *brag, or strut about.* There's no arrogance in love; it's never rude, crude, or indecent—it's not self-absorbed. Love isn't easily upset. Love doesn't tally wrongs or celebrate injustice; but truth—*yes, truth*—is love's delight! Love puts up with anything and everything that comes along; it trusts, hopes, and endures no matter what.

Renew Your Love

"What happens when we live God's way? He brings gifts into our lives, much the same way that fruit appears in an orchard" (Galatians 5:22 THE MESSAGE).

This is one of my favorite passages in the Bible! Galatians 5:22–23 explains how we move from broken to beautiful, how we rise and renew: "The Holy Spirit produces this kind of fruit in our lives: love, joy, peace, patience, kindness, goodness, faithfulness, gentleness, and self-control."

Over the next nine days, we're going to look more closely at these gifts—this fruit—the evidence that God's Spirit is working in us and through us. We're going to look at what He does (His part) and what we do (our part)—how we participate in the process of producing "much fruit" (John 15:5).

As Paul prayed for the first believers—and for us: "May you always be filled with the fruit of your salvation—the righteous character produced in your life by Jesus Christ—for this will bring much glory and praise to God" (Philippians 1:11).

We start with *love*.

Such a powerful word. Such a powerful feeling.

But love is so much more than a feeling.

As we've just read, love is the "fruit" or evidence of God's Spirit living in us—and it's something we can cultivate, something we can nurture and grow.

In my own life I've found it crucial to remember again and again that love is also an act of the will. Something we can choose.

Feelings may come and go, but we can choose to love God and to love others, regardless of how our feelings fluctuate. We can choose to think loving things and do loving things each and every day.

We can choose to walk in love, speak in love, live in love.

We can renew this love in our hearts again and again by choosing it again and again—even when it's hard. Even when it doesn't come naturally.

We can do it supernaturally—because we have the Spirit of God living in us and loving through us.

think on it

In John 13:34–35, Jesus said, "So now I am giving you a new commandment: Love each other. Just as I have loved you, you should love each other. Your love for one another will prove to the world that you are my disciples." How have you seen this demonstrated? How have you seen God's people show love for one another and for the world?

How have you shown this kind of love?

Where is there room for growth in God's people (in the church) today? What about in you personally?

think on it

Ephesians 5:1–2 says, "Imitate God, therefore, in everything you do, because you are his dear children. Live a life filled with love, following the example of Christ." What do you think "a life filled with love" looks like?

What are some specific ways you can follow the example of Jesus? What steps can you take and what choices can you make to choose love and to renew your love for Him and for others today?

Act on It

With the Spirit of God in you, you can be the very definition of love found in 1 Corinthians 13:4–7. So write your name in place of the word *love* in the verses below. Make it a prayer! Read it aloud every day this week and look for ways you can live it.

________________ is patient and kind. ________________ is not jealous or boastful or proud or rude. ________________ does not demand her own way. ________________ is not irritable, and ________________ keeps no record of being wronged. ________________ does not rejoice about injustice but rejoices whenever the truth wins out. ________________ never gives up, ________________ never loses faith, ________________ is always hopeful, and ________________ endures through every circumstance.

THREE THINGS WILL LAST FOREVER—FAITH, HOPE, AND LOVE—AND THE GREATEST OF THESE IS LOVE.

1 CORINTHIANS 13:13

Day
20

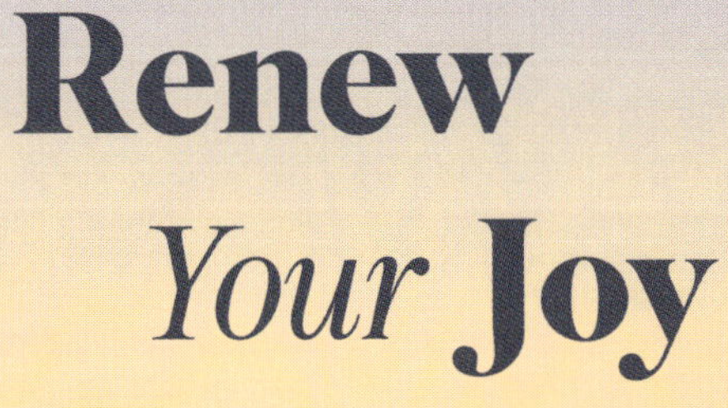

Renew *Your* Joy

Always be full of joy in the Lord. I say it again—rejoice!

PHILIPPIANS 4:4

The Lord is my strength and shield. I trust him with all my heart. He helps me, and my heart is filled with joy. I burst out in songs of thanksgiving.

PSALM 28:7

Psalm 40:8

I take joy in doing your will, my God, for your instructions are written on my heart.

Psalm 51:12

Restore to me the joy of your salvation, and make me willing to obey you.

Psalm 9:2

I will be filled with joy because of you. I will sing praises to your name, O Most High.

Psalm 63:5

You satisfy me more than the richest feast. I will praise you with songs of joy.

Psalm 30:11

You have turned my mourning into joyful dancing. You have taken away my clothes of mourning and clothed me with joy.

Psalm 16:11
THE VOICE

You direct me on the path that leads to *a beautiful* life. As I walk with You, the pleasures are never-ending, and I know true joy *and contentment.*

Psalm 63:7

Because you are my helper, I sing for joy in the shadow of your wings.

Psalm 5:11

Let all who take refuge in you rejoice; let them sing joyful praises forever. Spread your protection over them, that all who love your name may be filled with joy.

Renew Your Joy

The Bible tells us of a time when God's people had abandoned His Word and His ways. They were living in disobedience, in rebellion, in sin. God warned them over and over about the consequences of their choices, but they didn't listen. They ended up being conquered by an enemy nation, sold into slavery, and taken into exile far away from their homeland.

Many years later, when the people were finally released, they returned to find their cities in ruins, the walls broken and crumbling.

So you know that they did? They rebuilt.

They came together under the leadership of Nehemiah and Ezra and started with the walls (after all, there's no point rebuilding a city without any protection!).

It was hard work. They encountered all kinds of obstacles, faced all kinds of opposition. But with God's help they overcame it.

When the walls were finished, the leaders called everyone to come together for a dedication ceremony, a celebration.

Some people had a hard time with that. They still felt guilt and shame over the past. They couldn't help but remember how good things had been before they messed it all up. They couldn't help but think about how far they still had to go—how much work it would take to rebuild not just their walls but their cities, their homes, their communities, their lives. How long before the whole country would really heal and recover?

That's when Nehemiah stepped up to give them a special word of encouragement: "Don't mourn or weep on such a day as this! . . . Go and celebrate. . . . Don't be dejected and sad, for the joy of the LORD is your strength!" (Nehemiah 8:9–10).

Even in our brokenness, we can experience joy. Even when the healing is still happening, even when it's a process, when it's taking time (and doesn't it always?), we can rejoice.

We're joyful because, no matter what, God is good. Because He loves us—even when we're broken. Even when it's all our fault.

We're joyful because we know that's not the end of the story—no matter what things look like, no matter how they feel. We know that God is at work even now, turning our brokenness into something beautiful.

He is our joy; He is our strength; He is our song (Exodus 15:2).

think on it

James 1:2–4 says, "Don't run from tests and hardships, brothers and sisters. *As difficult as they are, you will ultimately* find joy in them; if you embrace them, your faith will blossom under pressure *and teach you true patience* as you endure. *And true patience brought on by* endurance will equip you to complete the long journey *and cross the finish line*—mature, complete, and wanting nothing" (THE VOICE). What challenges—what tests or hardships—are you facing today? What things threaten to keep you from finding joy?

How can you "embrace" these things? Where can you find joy, when you're still in the process, when it's all very much a work in progress?

think on it

Where do you see your faith "blossoming" or growing? What are you learning?

Psalm 95:1–2 exclaims, "Come, let us sing to the Lord! Let us shout joyfully to the Rock of our salvation. Let us come to him with thanksgiving. Let us sing psalms of praise to him." Verses like these remind us that singing and joy often go hand in hand—when we sing, we're joyful; and when we're joyful, we sing. And Psalm 100:1 calls us to "make a joyful noise to the Lord" (ESV). It doesn't have to be an award-winning performance, just heartfelt and enthusiastic! How can you "make a joyful noise" and sing to the Lord today?

Act on It

Let's take our cue from Nehemiah's encouragement to God's people and not miss an opportunity to celebrate how good God is, how far He's brought us, and all that we've accomplished—by His grace, in His strength, for His glory—even in the midst of our brokenness. Even while we're still in the process.

Choose something in your life to celebrate, and plan a party! You can go big or small, host a little get-together for coffee with friends, schedule a special night out (or in), or throw a dance party in your living room, even if it's just you!

Once you have a plan, design an invitation below. Be sure to include the reason, the date, the time and place, and the dress code!

NOW ALL GLORY TO GOD, WHO IS ABLE TO KEEP YOU FROM FALLING AWAY AND WILL BRING YOU WITH GREAT JOY INTO HIS GLORIOUS PRESENCE.

JUDE V. 24

Day
21

Renew *Your* Peace

I am leaving you with a gift—peace of mind and heart. And the peace I give is a gift the world cannot give. So don't be troubled or afraid.

JOHN 14:27

Don't fret or worry. Instead of worrying, pray. Let petitions and praises shape your worries into prayers, letting God know your concerns. Before you know it, a sense of God's wholeness, everything coming together for good, will come and settle you down. It's wonderful what happens when Christ displaces worry at the center of your life.

PHILIPPIANS 4:6–7 THE MESSAGE

1 Corinthians 1:3	May God our Father and the Lord Jesus Christ give you grace and peace.
Psalm 29:11	The LORD gives his people strength. The LORD blesses them with peace.
Philippians 4:7 *AMP*	And the peace of God [that peace which reassures the heart, that peace] which transcends all understanding, [that peace which] stands guard over your hearts and your minds in Christ Jesus [is yours].
Ephesians 4:3	Make every effort to keep yourselves united in the Spirit, binding yourselves together with peace.
Colossians 3:15	And let the peace that comes from Christ rule in your hearts. For as members of one body you are called to live in peace. And always be thankful.
Romans 16:20	The God of peace will soon crush Satan under your feet.
John 16:33	I have told you all this so that you may have peace in me. Here on earth you will have many trials and sorrows. But take heart, because I have overcome the world.

A NOTE FROM *Candace*

Renew Your Peace

People ask me all the time how I stay so positive and cheerful and optimistic, especially in a world where bad things happen. Sometimes the headlines are really scary. There's a lot of pain and suffering all around us—sometimes in our own homes and in our own hearts. It's true. I'm not immune to any of that.

I stay positive not because my life is perfect or pain-free—it isn't. I'm cheerful not because I don't have anything to be sad about—I do. I'm optimistic not because I keep my head in the sand, clueless to what's going on—I don't.

I stay positive because I trust the Word of God.

I believe what God says.

And He says that no matter what it looks like or how it feels, He is on His throne. He is in control. He cares for you and for me.

He says He will protect us. He will provide for us. He will strengthen us. He will heal us. He will lead us and guide us.

Somehow He will work all things—*all* things—together for our good (Romans 8:28).

That's what I stand on. That's what I believe with every fiber of my being.

I believe.

And it brings me peace. A peace "which transcends all understanding" (Philippians 4:7 AMP). A peace that nothing can shake.

I have my moments—I'm human. I feel frustrated or discouraged or worried or afraid. But I can't stay in that place. I can't continue to dwell on those things.

Paul says in Philippians 4:8–9, "Whatever is true, whatever is noble, whatever is right, whatever is pure, whatever is lovely, whatever is admirable—if anything is excellent or praiseworthy—think about such things. Whatever you have learned or received or heard from me, or seen in me—put it into practice. And the God of peace will be with you" (NIV).

So that's what I strive to do. That's what I take to heart. That's what I focus on. The God of peace. And His gift of peace. A gift He offers to you too.

think on it

What challenges your sense of peace or tries to rob you of it?

Where do you most need the God of peace—the gift of peace—in your heart, your mind, or your life today?

Speaking to God, the prophet Isaiah said, "You will keep in perfect peace all who trust in you, all whose thoughts are fixed on you!" (Isaiah 26:3). How can you fix your thoughts on Him? When you're tempted to become anxious, worried, angry, or afraid, what can you do to refocus and renew your peace?

think on it

Psalm 119:165 says, "Great peace have those who love your law, and nothing can make them stumble" (NIV). How does loving God's Word and living in obedience to Him bring us peace or protect our peace?

Romans 5:1 tells us, "We have peace with God because of what Jesus Christ our Lord has done for us." Our brokenness and sin are no longer a barrier between us and Him. Guilt and shame have no more power over us. Neither does worry or fear. We have been renewed and restored by the power of His Spirit. How does being at peace with God help us live in peace with others?

Act on It

Remember what Philippians 4:6–7 says: "Don't worry about anything; instead, pray about everything. Tell God what you need, and thank him for all he has done. Then you will experience God's peace."

Use the space below to make a list of things that are worrying you or weighing on you—but as you write them, turn them into prayers and praises. Start with phrases like "Thank You, God, that You know _____, that You care for _____, that You provide for _____, that You protect _____. Thank You for being _____, for preparing _____, for working in _____. I trust You to _____. I trust You with _____."

When you're finished, hold all of these things up to God and release them to Him. Let Him carry them for you because He cares for you (1 Peter 5:7).

THINGS WORRYING AND WEIGHING ON ME	PRAYERS AND PRAISES

NOW MAY THE LORD OF PEACE HIMSELF GIVE YOU HIS PEACE AT ALL TIMES AND IN EVERY SITUATION. THE LORD BE WITH YOU ALL.

2 THESSALONIANS 3:16

Day
22

Renew *Your* Patience

Rejoice in our confident hope. Be patient in trouble, and keep on praying.

ROMANS 12:12

I waited patiently for the LORD to help me, and he turned to me and heard my cry. He lifted me out of the pit of despair, out of the mud and the mire. He set my feet on solid ground and steadied me as I walked along. He has given me a new song to sing, a hymn of praise to our God. Many will see what he has done and be amazed. They will put their trust in the LORD.

PSALM 40:1–3

Psalm 27:14

Wait patiently for the LORD. Be brave and courageous. Yes, wait patiently for the LORD.

Romans 12:12
THE MESSAGE

Don't burn out; keep yourselves fueled and aflame.
Be alert servants of the Master, cheerfully expectant.
Don't quit in hard times; pray all the harder. Help needy Christians; be inventive in hospitality.

1 Thessalonians 5:14–15
THE MESSAGE

Gently encourage the stragglers, and reach out for the exhausted, pulling them to their feet. Be patient with each person, attentive to individual needs. And be careful that when you get on each other's nerves you don't snap at each other. Look for the best in each other, and always do your best to bring it out.

Hebrews 10:36

Patient endurance is what you need now, so that you will continue to do God's will. Then you will receive all that he has promised.

Romans 15:5–6

May God, who gives this patience and encouragement, help you live in complete harmony with each other, as is fitting for followers of Christ Jesus. Then all of you can join together with one voice, giving praise and glory to God, the Father of our Lord Jesus Christ.

A NOTE FROM
Candace

Renew Your Patience

Good things come to those who wait.

God things.

Blessings, miracles, and answers to prayer.

Open doors, invitations, and opportunities.

Divine wisdom, direction, and provision.

Supernatural inspiration, motivation, and encouragement.

Renewed courage and strength, renewed hope and faith.

I'm not saying it's easy to wait. But even when we can't see it, even when we can't feel it, even when we can't believe it—God is at work.

He's at work in our hearts and lives and in the hearts and lives of everyone around us. He's at work in our schools and our workplaces, in our churches and our communities, in our nation and the nations of the world.

He is up to all kinds of good.

Often the biggest part of our job—of the work He has called us to do—is to be patient, to look to Him and trust Him to do what He does best. Trust Him and not run out ahead of Him. Let Him open hearts and minds, let Him open doors—and not try to force our way through. Rely on His Spirit, not our own wisdom or strength, to lead the way.

And we need to realize that sometimes the result of our waiting won't feel good. The answer we get won't always be the one we wanted, but that doesn't mean God isn't working. Because we know that God is good, we can trust that the result, whether we wanted it or not, is best.

I remember being a very impatient teenager. (I think most of us are pretty impatient at that age.) But if there's one thing that life has taught me over and over again, it's the value of being patient, of waiting on God's perfect timing. Trusting in Him. Resting in Him.

So many times I've seen Him work in amazing ways I never could have imagined—work all things together for my good (Romans 8:28).

While it hasn't been easy, I'm so thankful that God has helped me grow in patience. With the psalmist, I can exclaim: "Through my whole life (young and old), I have never witnessed God forsaking those who do right," those who love Him and trust Him (Psalm 37:25 THE VOICE).

That's why I practice patience—I cultivate patience—and yes, I pray for patience! I ask God to renew my patience whenever I run out. Because patience is more than a virtue. It's the spiritual fruit from a life that rests in Him.

How have you had opportunities to practice patience in your life? Where—or for whom or for what—have you had to wait?

When you look back now, can you see a plan or a purpose in the waiting? What have you learned in the process? How have you grown or matured? How has God met you in the waiting?

think on it

How has God been patient with you in your life? Where or how is He calling you to trust Him now and to be patient with yourself and/or others?

Romans 15:4 says, "The Scriptures give us hope and encouragement as we wait patiently for God's promises to be fulfilled." Which scriptures are encouraging your heart right now?

What can you do to remember and hold on to God's promises while you wait for their fulfillment?

Act on It

In the space below, write a prayer asking God to plant the seed of patience within you.

It takes time for good things to grow. There's so much that goes into the process, so many different factors that come into play. Practice patience by planting some seeds this week—in your garden, in a flowerpot, or even in a paper cup! (Remember those kindergarten science experiments?) Grow some flowers or fruits or vegetables, whatever you like!

As you nurture the seeds in good soil and with water and sunshine and fresh air, think about the ways God nurtures you. Think about His patience and tenderness with you. His willingness to wait for you—even as He constantly encourages you to flourish and grow. Ask God to help you find ways you can show some of that same patience to yourself and to others.

SO LET'S NOT GET TIRED OF DOING WHAT IS GOOD. AT JUST THE RIGHT TIME WE WILL REAP A HARVEST OF BLESSING IF WE DON'T GIVE UP.

GALATIANS 6:9

Day
23

Renew *Your* Kindness

Since you are all set apart by God, made holy and dearly loved, clothe yourselves with a holy way of life: *compassion, kindness, humility, gentleness, and patience.*

COLOSSIANS 3:12 THE VOICE

How kind the Lord *is! How good he is! So merciful, this God of ours!*

PSALM 116:5

Psalm 145:17	The LORD is righteous in everything he does; he is filled with kindness.
Ephesians 1:8	He has showered his kindness on us, along with all wisdom and understanding.
Ephesians 1:7	He is so rich in kindness and grace that he purchased our freedom with the blood of his Son and forgave our sins.
Ephesians 4:32	Be kind to each other, tenderhearted, forgiving one another, just as God through Christ has forgiven you.
Proverbs 3:3 AMP	Do not let mercy and kindness and truth leave you [instead let these qualities define you]; bind them [securely] around your neck, write them on the tablet of your heart.
2 Timothy 2:24	A servant of the Lord must not quarrel but must be kind to everyone, be able to teach, and be patient with difficult people.
Proverbs 31:26	When she speaks, her words are wise, and she gives instructions with kindness.
2 Corinthians 6:6	We prove ourselves by our purity, our understanding, our patience, our kindness, by the Holy Spirit within us, and by our sincere love.

A NOTE FROM Candace

Renew Your Kindness

If you look up the definition of *kindness* in the dictionary, you'll see some familiar words—*gentleness*, *goodness*, *faithfulness*, *love* (or *affection*)—already covered in the description of the fruit of the Spirit in Galatians 5:22–23.

So why does kindness get its own special mention?

Kindness takes things a step further, in a couple of really important ways.

For one thing, kindness goes beyond the discipline of doing the right thing at the right time for the right reason. Kindness makes a personal connection, an emotional connection. Kindness is truly sympathetic, even empathetic.

In other words, kindness really feels for others. Puts itself in their shoes and asks, "What would I need in this situation? How would I want to be treated?"

And—as the dictionary explains—kindness demonstrates a desire to be helpful. A willingness to get involved.

Then kindness takes action.

The Bible says God showed His kindness toward us when He sent His Son, Jesus, to the cross. He saw how lost we were in our sin, how hurt, how broken—and His heart went out to us.

He felt our pain. Literally. He shared that experience with us.

He was willing to help us—even though it would cost Him more than we can possibly understand or imagine. He took action. Look at what Titus 3 says:

> God our Savior and His overpowering love and kindness for humankind entered our world; He came to save us. It's not that *we earned it* by doing good works or righteous deeds; He came because He is merciful. He brought us *out of our old ways of living* to a new beginning through the washing of regeneration; and He made us completely new through the Holy Spirit. (vv. 4–5 THE VOICE)

And because He did that, we can show kindness too.

We can love others the way He loves us; we can feel their pain and want to help. We can be willing to get involved, even if it's at great personal cost. We can take action too. Not because others have somehow earned this kindness or deserve it, but because they need it. Just as desperately as we did—as desperately as we do.

think on it

Matthew 5:48 says, "Live out your God-created identity. Live generously and graciously toward others, the way God lives toward you" (THE MESSAGE). What are some of the ways God has shown kindness toward you?

What's one of the kindest things someone other than Jesus has done for you? What made it so memorable or meaningful?

think on it

Have you ever been surprised by a kindness that you didn't deserve or from someone you didn't expect? How did that impact you?

Have you ever had the opportunity to show kindness to someone who didn't deserve it? Was it hard to do? What motivated or inspired you?

How is God calling you to live "generously and graciously" right now? Who is He calling you to show kindness to?

Act on It

One of the best ways we can say thank you—to Jesus and to others—for the kindness we've received is to "pay it forward." Think about the people you encounter on a daily basis—in your home, your community, your church, your workplace—and brainstorm some ways you can bless them with kindness.

If this is something you already make a habit of, try to think of some new and different ideas—maybe some that stretch you a little or pull you a bit further outside your comfort zone. Draw gift tags below and jot those ideas down. Ask God to show you how and when to give these gifts—and to whom to give them—and to give you the grace to follow through.

LET US THINK OF WAYS TO MOTIVATE ONE ANOTHER TO ACTS OF LOVE AND GOOD WORKS.

HEBREWS 10:24

Day
24

Renew *Your* Goodness

The L*ORD* *has told you what is good, and this is what he requires of you: to do what is right, to love mercy, and to walk humbly with your God.*

MICAH 6:8

Be good to your servant, G*OD; be as good as your Word. Train me in good common sense; I'm thoroughly committed to living your way. Before I learned to answer you, I wandered all over the place, but now I'm in step with your Word. You are good, and the source of good; train me in your goodness.*

PSALM 119:65–68 THE MESSAGE

Romans 7:17–25; 8:2
THE MESSAGE

But I need something more! For if I know the law but still can't keep it, and if the power of sin within me keeps sabotaging my best intentions, I obviously need help! I realize that I don't have what it takes. I can will it, but I can't do it. I decide to do good, but I don't really do it; I decide not to do bad, but then I do it anyway. My decisions, such as they are, don't result in actions. Something has gone wrong deep within me and gets the better of me every time. It happens so regularly that it's predictable. The moment I decide to do good, sin is there to trip me up. I truly delight in God's commands, but it's pretty obvious that not all of me joins in that delight. Parts of me covertly rebel, and just when I least expect it, they take charge. I've tried everything and nothing helps. I'm at the end of my rope. Is there no one who can do anything for me? Isn't that the real question? The answer, thank God, is that Jesus Christ can and does. He acted to set things right in this life of contradictions where I want to serve God with all my heart and mind, but am pulled by the influence of sin to do something totally different. . . . A new power is in operation. The Spirit of life in Christ, like a strong wind, has magnificently cleared the air.

Psalm 23:6
ESV

Surely goodness and mercy shall follow me all the days of my life, and I shall dwell in the house of the LORD forever.

A NOTE FROM *Candace*

Renew Your Goodness

Sometimes it's a real struggle to do the right thing—to make good choices, to walk in faithful obedience to God's Word. Especially if we're trying to do it in our own strength, in our own power.

That's when our brokenness will come back to bite us every time.

But as I often told my daughter, Natasha, when she was a teenager, we don't have to do anything in our own strength. I even had Galatians 5:22–23 stenciled on her bedroom wall where she could see it first thing in the morning. It was to remind her that we have the Spirit of God living in us and working through us—and He helps us.

He empowers us to live a good life, an authentic life, a life of purity and integrity.

"When the Holy Spirit controls our lives he will produce this kind of fruit in us: love, joy, peace, patience, kindness, goodness, faithfulness, gentleness and self-control" (Galatians 5:22–23 TLB).

It seemed like Natasha's first instinct was always to rebel, to go against the grain, to do whatever she was asked not to do. She was tempted to take what seemed like the easy way out of any difficult situation.

But in the long run, it turns out that being bad is a lot harder than being (and doing) good. Making up lies or excuses—and then trying to remember them to keep them going or to cover them up. Living with the fear of getting caught, of being found out—running from the consequences, the guilt, and the shame.

It's hard work, as I told her, again and again!

But when you surrender to God's Spirit, His goodness flows through you.

Goodness breeds goodness.

You say good things. You do good things. You make good choices.

And God honors all that is good. He blesses it.

He blesses you—and everyone around you.

That's why the psalmist exclaimed: "Taste and see that the LORD is good. Oh, the joys of those who take refuge in him!" (Psalm 34:8).

I'm thrilled to say that Natasha has discovered this for herself. I love seeing her as a young adult being renewed by the power of the Spirit, choosing God, choosing goodness. It inspires me to keep doing the same!

think on it

How hard was it for you to make good choices when you were younger? Where did you struggle? What do you wish you could tell your younger self? What have you learned since then?

Where do you struggle now? What good things are hard to do or say? What good choices are hard to make? How is not making good choices even harder?

think on it

Titus 2:11–14 tells us, "God's readiness to give and forgive is now public. Salvation's available for everyone! We're being shown how to turn our backs on a godless, indulgent life, and how to take on a God-filled, God-honoring life. This new life is starting right now, and is whetting our appetites for the glorious day when our great God and Savior, Jesus Christ, appears. He offered himself as a sacrifice to free us from a dark, rebellious life into this good, pure life, making us a people he can be proud of, energetic in goodness" (THE MESSAGE). Ephesians 2:10 adds, "He has created us anew in Christ Jesus, so we can do the good things he planned for us long ago." What hope or motivation do you find in these verses?

What do you think it means to be "energetic in goodness"? What does that look like in your life?

Act on It

Psalm 34:14 urges us, "Turn away from evil and do good." Spend some time asking God to show you three things that are "evil"—unhealthy, unhelpful, unwholesome, unwise—that you need to turn from. And choose three "good" things—healthy, helpful, wholesome, wise—that you can do instead, good things He has called you to and planned for you to do.

I'm turning away from . . .

____

____

____

I'm choosing . . .

____

____

____

Ask Him to fill you with His Holy Spirit and empower you to do those good things today.

I LONG TO OBEY YOUR COMMANDMENTS!
RENEW MY LIFE WITH YOUR GOODNESS.

PSALM 119:40

Day
25

Renew *Your* Gentleness

Pursue righteousness and a godly life, along with faith, love, perseverance, and gentleness.

1 TIMOTHY 6:11

Worship Christ as Lord of your life. And if someone asks about your hope as a believer, always be ready to explain it. But do this in a gentle and respectful way.

1 PETER 3:15–16

Proverbs 15:1

A gentle answer deflects anger, but harsh words make tempers flare.

Colossians 3:12–13

Since God chose you to be the holy people he loves, you must clothe yourselves with tenderhearted mercy, kindness, humility, gentleness, and patience. Make allowance for each other's faults, and forgive anyone who offends you. Remember, the Lord forgave you, so you must forgive others.

1 Peter 3:3–4
THE MESSAGE

What matters is not your outer appearance—the styling of your hair, the jewelry you wear, the cut of your clothes—but your inner disposition. Cultivate inner beauty, the gentle, gracious kind that God delights in.

1 Peter 3:4 AMP

Let it be [the inner beauty of] the hidden person of the heart, with the imperishable quality *and* unfading charm of a gentle and peaceful spirit, [one that is calm and self-controlled, not overanxious, but serene and spiritually mature] which is very precious in the sight of God.

James 3:17–18
THE MESSAGE

Real wisdom, God's wisdom, begins with a holy life and is characterized by getting along with others. It is gentle and reasonable, overflowing with mercy and blessings, not hot one day and cold the next, not two-faced. You can develop a healthy, robust community that lives right with God and enjoy its results *only* if you do the hard work of getting along with each other, treating each other with dignity and honor.

A NOTE FROM *Candace*

Renew Your Gentleness

If there's anything recent years have taught us, it's how much we need the Spirit of God to help us love one another—despite our differences—and express ourselves with gentleness and respect.

We just can't do it on our own.

We don't even realize, sometimes, how harsh we sound.

But emotions run high—and hot. Our voices rise or our fingers fly across the keyboard, composing an email or post or text. And what comes after is hardly ever "gracious," "good," "wholesome," "encouraging," or "beneficial," "building others up" (Colossians 4:6; Ephesians 4:29, various translations).

Proverbs 18:21 says, "The tongue can bring death or life; those who love to talk will reap the consequences."

Yikes!

Believe it or not, for some of us—me included—the battle is just as big in our self-talk. We have real trouble being gentle when we talk to ourselves or about ourselves—when we think about our past, our successes or failures, our to-do lists (what we have or haven't accomplished), or we have trouble being gentle when we look in the mirror.

I try to remember what the Scripture says about how I should speak to (or about) myself and to (or about) others: "The words of the reckless pierce like swords, but the tongue of the wise brings healing" (Proverbs 12:18 NIV). "Gentle words are a tree of life" (Proverbs 15:4).

And I remind myself how gentle God is with me—how unfailingly kind and gracious and loving. How patient.

I can be that way, too, with myself and with others—if I have His Spirit living within me. And I do. With His help, I can speak words of life and hope and healing.

So can you!

think on it

How would you describe what the word *gentle* means? What images come to mind? What thoughts or feelings?

Someone once defined *gentleness* not as weakness (which it's sometimes mistaken for) but as power under control. How would you describe the difference? (Hint: The key is in the choosing, in having or making a choice, rather than being powerless or out of control.)

think on it

Are there people in your life—people you have known—who come to mind when you think of gentleness? What is it about them? What is it that they say or do that communicates gentleness to you? What do you respect or admire about them? How do you feel when you're with them?

Where do you need a renewed spirit of gentleness in your own life today? What would that look like? Who would it impact? How would it influence what you do or what you say?

Act on It

In *The Message*, Colossians 3:14 is paraphrased like this: "Regardless of what else you put on, wear love. It's your basic, all-purpose garment. Never be without it."

Today, find something soft to wear—fuzzy socks or a silky scarf or a well-worn T-shirt, sweatshirt, or cozy sweater. Every time you brush up against the fabric, let it remind you to be gentle with yourself and with others. Gentle in your words, gentle in your tone, gentle in your attitude and approach, gentle in your actions.

Are you in conflict with someone today? (If not, think of a conflict you've experienced in the past.) In the space below, write down a strategy of gentleness for addressing the person and the issue you have. Then ask God to help you lead with gentleness.

PUT ON A HEART OF COMPASSION, KINDNESS, HUMILITY, GENTLENESS, AND PATIENCE [WHICH HAS THE POWER TO ENDURE WHATEVER INJUSTICE OR UNPLEASANTNESS COMES, WITH GOOD TEMPER]; BEARING GRACIOUSLY WITH ONE ANOTHER.

COLOSSIANS 3:12–13 AMP

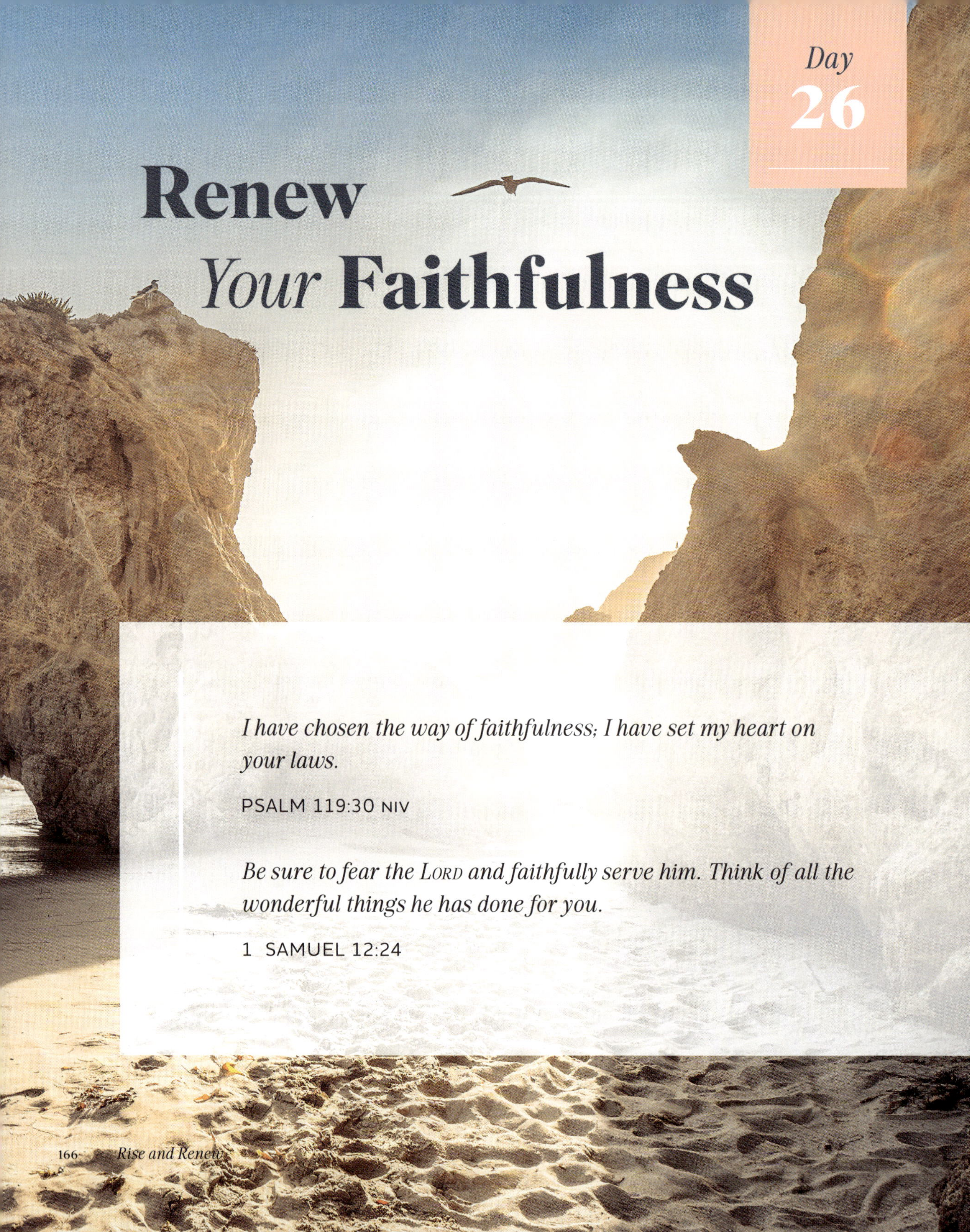

Day 26

Renew *Your* Faithfulness

I have chosen the way of faithfulness; I have set my heart on your laws.

PSALM 119:30 NIV

Be sure to fear the L*ORD* *and faithfully serve him. Think of all the wonderful things he has done for you.*

1 SAMUEL 12:24

1 Kings 8:61	May you be completely faithful to the LORD our God. May you always obey his decrees and commands, just as you are doing today.
John 8:31	Jesus said to the people who believed in him, "You are truly my disciples if you remain faithful to my teachings."
2 Timothy 3:14	You must remain faithful to the things you have been taught.
Luke 16:10	If you are faithful in little things, you will be faithful in large ones.
Psalm 149:5	Let the faithful rejoice that he honors them. Let them sing for joy.
Hebrews 3:14	For if we are faithful to the end, trusting God just as firmly as when we first believed, we will share in all that belongs to Christ.
2 Timothy 4:7	I have fought the good fight, I have finished the race, and I have remained faithful.

Renew Your Faithfulness

Beginning to end, the Bible is full of verses that tell us God is faithful—constant, loyal, committed, devoted—to us. And because *He* is faithful, He calls *us* to be faithful—to dedicate our hearts and lives to Him, just as He has dedicated Himself to us.

Sometimes that means answering His call—using the gifts He's given us to do the work He's given us to do—even when it's hard. Even when it's challenging.

When it seems extraordinary *and* when it seems ordinary.

When it's super exciting and when it's . . . well . . . boring.

When we have lots of cheerleaders rooting for us and (although it may not make sense to those around us) when we don't feel their love or appreciation or support.

Because we love Him—and He loves us—we say yes!

We show up.

We put in the time.

We give it our best.

And we are blessed.

We experience the power of the Holy Spirit, working in and through us, giving us the grace and strength we need to be faithful, to keep on keeping on.

We learn so much more about who God is and who we are and where He is at work in the world around us.

And we get to be part of that work! Even if our part doesn't seem very significant—because, as they say in show business, there are no small parts. Every single one is important. He could tell the story—His story—without us. But He's chosen to invite us to play a part.

And playing our part—doing our part of God's work in the world—is where, ultimately, we will find our greatest satisfaction and fulfillment. It's where we will find joy and peace and purpose. It's the role of a lifetime!

Our faithfulness, day by day, is just a tiny reflection of His own.

think on it

Lamentations 3:22–23 says, "The faithful love of the LORD never ends! His mercies never cease. Great is His faithfulness." Where do you see God's faithfulness in your life?

Where is God calling you to be faithful? What has He asked you personally to do, right now, in this season of your life?

think on it

What does faithfulness look like for you? What does it mean—specifically to you in your circumstances—to answer His call?

How is your heart in all this? Your attitude? Your behavior? Are there any decisions or adjustments you need to make? Any steps you need to take? Pray and ask God to help you with this.

Act on It

Look at some of the many synonyms for *faithful* in the list below. Circle three that describe who God is to you and fill in the blanks, adding a note about why you chose each word. Then underline (or circle in a different color) three words that you want to describe you. Copy them in the blanks and explain what they mean to you.

- loyal
- constant
- true
- devoted
- unchanging
- unwavering
- enduring
- steadfast
- good
- true-blue
- true-hearted
- unswerving
- dedicated
- devoted
- sure
- trustworthy
- dutiful
- loving
- conscientious
- honest
- devout
- upright
- honorable
- dependable
- reliable
- obedient
- resolute
- committed
- hard-core
- tried-and-true
- trusted
- truthful

Who God is to me:

____

____

____

Who I want to be:

____

____

____

LET US HOLD TIGHTLY WITHOUT WAVERING TO THE HOPE WE AFFIRM, FOR GOD CAN BE TRUSTED TO KEEP HIS PROMISE.

HEBREWS 10:23

Day
27

Renew *Your* Self-Control

Blessed [inwardly peaceful, spiritually secure, worthy of respect] are the gentle [the kind-hearted, the sweet-spirited, the self-controlled].

MATTHEW 5:5 AMP

Dear brothers and sisters, you have no obligation to do what your sinful nature urges you to do.

ROMANS 8:12

Romans 6:12–13

Do not let sin control the way you live; do not give in to sinful desires. Do not let any part of your body become an instrument of evil to serve sin. Instead, give yourselves completely to God, for you were dead, but now you have new life. So use your whole body as an instrument to do what is right for the glory of God.

2 Peter 1:3–4

By his divine power, God has given us everything we need for living a godly life. We have received all of this by coming to know him, the one who called us to himself by means of his marvelous glory and excellence. And because of his glory and excellence, he has given us great and precious promises. These are the promises that enable you to share his divine nature and escape the world's corruption caused by human desires.

1 Peter 1:13–16
THE MESSAGE

So roll up your sleeves, get your head in the game, be totally ready to receive the gift that's coming when Jesus arrives. Don't lazily slip back into those old grooves of evil, doing just what you feel like doing. You didn't know any better then; you do now. As obedient children, let yourselves be pulled into a way of life shaped by God's life, a life energetic and blazing with holiness. God said, "I am holy; you be holy."

2 Peter 1:5–8

Make every effort to respond to God's promises. Supplement your faith with a generous provision of moral excellence, and moral excellence with knowledge, and knowledge with self-control, and self-control with patient endurance, and patient endurance with godliness, and godliness with brotherly affection, and brotherly affection with love for everyone. The more you grow like this, the more productive and useful you will be in your knowledge of our Lord Jesus Christ.

Renew Your Self-Control

Self-control. I have to admit that it's one of my biggest challenges, my biggest battles. Sometimes—okay, often—my human nature threatens to get the best of me.

Things go wrong and I lose my temper—I get angry and upset. I try not to let it out in front of other people, so I head to my car or my closet at home, where I can be by myself. And that's where I boil over. I cry or punch a pillow or sometimes I scream to no one or to God. We all have some version of a temper tantrum, even as adults.

I mean, I have to laugh when I think of how ridiculous it is . . . a grown woman throwing a tantrum like a toddler. But it also makes me sad that I don't have more self-control. That, even privately, I'm giving way to anger. I'm doing and saying things that aren't honoring to God.

And that's not the only area where self-control is an issue for me.

I could make excuses. I could minimize and rationalize and explain it all away. I could compare my behavior to others in a way that makes me look like a saint. Or I could beat myself up over it. Wallow in guilt and shame. Sigh helplessly over my brokenness and my humanity and throw my hands up in defeat.

But I don't want to do any of those things.

Because I believe—I really, really believe—that Jesus died on the cross for all my sin. And that He's set me free from the power of sin.

Because of Him, I'm not held captive to my old nature. I'm not bound by my brokenness.

I believe that Jesus has something better for me.

"Anyone who belongs to Christ has become a new person. The old life is gone; a new life has begun!" (2 Corinthians 5:17).

God has sent His Spirit to live within me. He has given me the power to choose how I respond to the challenges I face.

His grace is teaching me every day how "to say 'No' to ungodliness and worldly passions, and to live self-controlled, upright and godly lives in this present age" (Titus 2:12 NIV).

My part is to keep learning, keep listening, and keep saying no to my flesh and yes to Him.

Where do you battle for self-control? In which areas do you feel most weak or vulnerable?

What are your triggers? What specific situations or circumstances particularly challenge you?

think on it

How do you typically—or habitually—respond? What does losing control look like for you?

How do you want to respond? What do you think God wants you to do? What would be a victory for you?

Who can you share your struggles with? Who might be a source of accountability, encouragement, and support for you?

Act on It

Proverbs 25:28 observes, "Like a city that is broken down and without walls [leaving it unprotected] is a man who has no self-control over his spirit [and sets himself up for trouble]" (AMP). But 2 Thessalonians 3:3 says, "The Lord is faithful; he will strengthen you and guard you from the evil one." With His help, you can rebuild the walls that protect you—your heart, your mind, your spirit, your life, your work, your family.

Think of a specific area in which you're asking God to help you develop more self-control. Picture it in the empty space below. Then add some bricks—draw them in—and write on them positive steps you can take, choices you can make. (Alternately, you can fill the space with scriptures that speak to you on this subject.)

DON'T BE DISCOURAGED, FOR I AM YOUR GOD. I WILL STRENGTHEN YOU AND HELP YOU. I WILL HOLD YOU UP WITH MY VICTORIOUS RIGHT HAND.

ISAIAH 41:10

Day

28

Renew *Your* Inspiration

The whole earth is filled with awe at your wonders; where morning dawns, where evening fades, you call forth songs of joy.

PSALM 65:8 NIV

O Lord, our Lord, your majestic name fills the earth! Your glory is higher than the heavens. . . . When I look at the night sky and see the work of your fingers—the moon and the stars you set in place—what are mere mortals that you should think about them, human beings that you should care for them? Yet you made them only a little lower than God and crowned them with glory and honor.

PSALM 8:1, 3–5

Psalm 77:14

You are the God of great wonders! You demonstrate your awesome power among the nations.

Psalm 145:2
AMP

Every day I will bless You and lovingly praise You; yes, [with awe-inspired reverence] I will praise Your name forever and ever.

Psalm 40:5

O LORD my God, you have performed many wonders for us. Your plans for us are too numerous to list. You have no equal. If I tried to recite all your wonderful deeds, I would never come to the end of them.

Psalm 33:18
AMP

Behold, the eye of the LORD is upon those who fear Him [and worship Him with awe-inspired reverence and obedience], on those who hope [confidently] in His compassion *and* lovingkindness.

Psalm 33:8
THE VOICE

Let all people stand in awe of the Eternal; let every man, woman, and child live in wonder of Him.

Romans 11:36

For everything comes from him and exists by his power and is intended for his glory. All glory to him forever! Amen.

A NOTE FROM *Candace*

Renew Your Inspiration

Sometimes our world gets too small. We put our heads down so we can focus on the task at hand—and we completely lose perspective. We're so busy problem-solving that all we can see are the problems. We get lost in the details, in the dailyness of life, and forget the bigger picture.

The solution to this problem? Make it a point to pause every so often and take a deep breath—in and out. And look up:

"I lift my eyes to you, O God" (Psalm 123:1).

Look up.

"Look up into the heavens. Who created all the stars? He brings them out . . . one after another, calling each by its name. Because of his great power and incomparable strength, not a single one is missing" (Isaiah 40:26).

Look up and then look around at the glory and majesty of God's creation, the infinite variety, the intricate detail in all that He has made.

Look not only at the staggering beauty of a sunrise or sunset or the stars in the night sky but also at the fields and forests, the mountains, the ocean—and all the amazing creatures who make their homes there.

Look at all the art and literature and music God has inspired and given us the ability to create. All the gifts of science and medicine and technology.

Think about the world of your senses—all that you can see or hear, touch, smell or taste. God created these things too.

"Great is the LORD! He is most worthy of praise! No one can measure his greatness. Let each generation tell its children of your mighty acts; let them proclaim your power. I will meditate on your majestic, glorious splendor and your wonderful miracles. . . . I will proclaim your greatness" (Psalm 145:3–6).

Take another deep breath, and remember that this same God created you—loves you, cares for you, protects you, and provides for you!

Be encouraged!

Be inspired!

Nothing you will ever face is too difficult for God.

He is in control.

And He does all things well.

think on it

In 1 Corinthians 16:14 it says, "Let everything you do be done in love [motivated and inspired by God's love for us]" (AMP). Practically speaking, how does God's love motivate you and inspire what you do?

Where do you encounter that motivation and inspiration? How do you experience it?

How is love (love for others, your love for God, and God's love for you) different from other kinds of motivation or inspiration?

What do you do "for the love of God"—in response to His love for you—that maybe you wouldn't do for any other reason? How does His love keep you going when life gets hard?

Act on It

One of the most beautiful and beloved hymns in all the world, "How Great Thou Art," was inspired by the words of Psalm 8 (see the verses at the beginning of this day's reading) reflecting on the beauty of God's creation. Take a few moments to listen to this hymn—there are *thousands* of versions online—and let your heart sing along. Then look for a way to incorporate one of the following activities into your schedule this week. Underline, circle, or highlight your plan:

- Get up early to watch a sunrise.
- Go for a walk by the lake or on the beach or in the forest, or go for a hike in the mountains (whatever creation you have access to, whatever inspires you!).
- Eat a meal outside at a restaurant or on your patio, or take a picnic to the park.
- Choose a night to go stargazing—visit a planetarium, pull out a telescope (if you have one), or just lie on a blanket in your backyard and look up!
- Go outside and take a picture of a rainbow, a cloud, a gorgeous sunset, a bird or a butterfly or a deer—again, whatever nature you encounter in your daily life. Make it a scavenger hunt if you like! Ask friends to join you and share what you discover together.
- Watch a nature show or documentary.
- Volunteer at an animal shelter or wildlife habitat, join a community cleanup, or host a fundraiser for an organization that cares for God's creation.
- Write your own "hymn" of praise—a song or poem—inspired by what you see.

SING SONGS TO GOD, SING OUT! SING TO OUR KING, SING PRAISE! HE'S LORD OVER EARTH, SO SING YOUR BEST SONGS TO GOD.

PSALM 47:6–7 THE MESSAGE

Renew *Your* Education

Wise men and women are always learning, always listening for fresh insights.

PROVERBS 18:15 THE MESSAGE

Ever since I first heard of your strong faith in the Lord Jesus and your love for God's people everywhere, I have not stopped thanking God for you. I pray for you constantly, asking God, the glorious Father of our Lord Jesus Christ, to give you spiritual wisdom and insight so that you might grow in your knowledge of God.

EPHESIANS 1:15–17

Colossians 3:10	Put on your new nature, and be renewed as you learn to know your Creator and become like him.
Romans 12:2	Don't copy the behavior and customs of this world, but let God transform you into a new person by changing the way you think. Then you will learn to know God's will for you, which is good and pleasing and perfect.
Proverbs 2:6	For the LORD grants wisdom! From his mouth come knowledge and understanding.
Colossians 2:3	In him lie hidden all the treasures of wisdom and knowledge.
Proverbs 2:10	For wisdom will enter your heart, and knowledge will fill you with joy.
2 Peter 1:5–8 THE MESSAGE	So don't lose a minute in building on what you've been given, complementing your basic faith with good character, spiritual understanding, alert discipline, passionate patience, reverent wonder, warm friendliness, and generous love, each dimension fitting into and developing the others. With these qualities active and growing in your lives, no grass will grow under your feet, no day will pass without its reward as you mature in your experience of our Master Jesus.

Renew Your Education

We're coming to the end of our thirty-day journey together, but we'll never get to the end of our adventure of faith.

We'll never get to the end of God—or His call for us to rise and renew.

Each new day is a new opportunity to experience His healing love, His resurrection power, His extravagant mercy and grace.

His abundant joy.

His perfect peace.

There will always, always be more to discover. More we can learn. More areas we can grow.

"This is GOD's Message, the God who made earth, made it livable and lasting, known everywhere as GOD: 'Call to me and I will answer you. I'll tell you marvelous and wondrous things that you could never figure out on your own'" (Jeremiah 33:2–3 THE MESSAGE).

"The LORD says, 'I will guide you along the best pathway for your life. I will advise you and watch over you'" (Psalm 32:8).

Isn't that amazing?

God Himself is our Counselor, our Mentor, our Teacher, our Guide. No matter what challenges we encounter or what obstacles we face, no matter what twists and turns our journey takes, we can trust His leading.

We can look for the learning.

We can grow wiser, stronger, deeper.

We can grow healed and whole and holy.

God is faithful. He promises that He will never give up on us, never hold out on us. He will finish what He started—the wonderful work that He began in us and through us (Philippians 1:6).

Our job is to keep coming to Him with an open heart, an open mind, a teachable spirit, and a willingness to learn—and to rise up and put into practice what we have learned—each new day.

think on it

Take a few moments to flip back through the pages of this book and reflect on what you have learned so far in our time together. See if you can list your top three takeaways or aha moments.

In Luke 11:28, Jesus said, "Blessed are all who hear the word of God and put it into practice." How have you been putting what you've learned into practice? Where do you see yourself rising up and being renewed? What steps have you taken, big or small?

think on it

What's been your biggest challenge on this journey? Where have you struggled? What are you still working on?

What else do you want—or need—to learn, in any area of your life? Physically? Mentally? Spiritually? In your relationships, in your career, in your ministry? Where would you like to go? Where would you like to grow?

Act on It

Spend some time in prayer about the next steps in your journey. Pray about the things you want or need to learn, the ways that—by God's grace, in His power, and for His glory—you'd love to rise and renew next. Now make a plan to do your part.

Choose one thing. Name it. Describe what it looks like and what it means to you—why it's important. Figure out what resources you'll need—who you can talk to and where you can go for inspiration, accountability, or practical help and support. Jot down the first few steps you will take. And schedule them in your planner.

MAY GOD GIVE YOU MORE AND MORE GRACE AND PEACE AS YOU GROW IN YOUR KNOWLEDGE OF GOD AND JESUS OUR LORD.

2 PETER 1:2

Day
30

Renew *Your* Determination

I am determined to keep your decrees to the very end.

PSALM 119:112

God blesses those who patiently endure testing and temptation. Afterward they will receive the crown of life that God has promised to those who love him.

JAMES 1:12

2 Corinthians 4:16–17

That is why we never give up. . . . For our present troubles are small and won't last very long. Yet they produce for us a glory that vastly outweighs them and will last forever!

1 Corinthians 9:26
THE MESSAGE

I don't know about you, but I'm running hard for the finish line. I'm giving it everything I've got.

Philippians 3:12–14
THE MESSAGE

I'm not saying that I have this all together, that I have it made. But I am well on my way, reaching out for Christ, who has so wondrously reached out for me. Friends, don't get me wrong: By no means do I count myself an expert in all of this, but I've got my eye on the goal, where God is beckoning us onward—to Jesus. I'm off and running, and I'm not turning back.

Hebrews 12:2–3
THE MESSAGE

Keep your eyes on Jesus, who both began and finished this race we're in. Study how he did it. Because he never lost sight of where he was headed—that exhilarating finish in and with God—he could put up with anything along the way: Cross, shame, whatever. And now he's there, in the place of honor, right alongside God. When you find yourselves flagging in your faith, go over that story again, item by item, that long litany of hostility he plowed through. That will shoot adrenaline into your souls!

Ephesians 1:15–19
THE MESSAGE

When I heard of the solid trust you have in the Master Jesus and your outpouring of love to all the followers of Jesus, I couldn't stop thanking God for you—every time I prayed, I'd think of you and give thanks. But I do more than thank. I ask—ask the God of our Master, Jesus Christ, the God of glory—to make you intelligent and discerning in knowing him personally, your eyes focused and clear, so that you can see exactly what it is he is calling you to do, grasp the immensity of this glorious way of life he has for his followers, oh, the utter extravagance of his work in us who trust him—endless energy, boundless strength!

Renew Your Determination

This is the great adventure to which God has called us: to rise up out of the ashes, rise up out of our brokenness, out of our sinful human nature, our grief and pain, our failure and defeat.

Rise up!

Rise up in the power of the resurrection.

Rise up in redemption, in forgiveness, in hope, and in healing.

Rise up in courage, faith, and newness of life.

Rise up in purpose, in passion, and in wisdom.

Rise up in worship. Rise up in grace. Rise up in abundance.

Rise up and renew.

Renew your heart, your mind, your strength.

Renew your spirit—and produce the fruit of God's Spirit working in and through you: love, joy, peace, patience, kindness, goodness, gentleness, faithfulness, and self-control.

Renew your inspiration, your education, and your determination.

Friend, you've come too far to stop now. You've overcome so many obstacles and accomplished so many amazing things along the way.

In 1 Peter 1:6 it says, "Be truly glad. There is wonderful joy ahead."

Abounding joy! Tremendous joy! Relentless joy!

So don't give up. No matter what.

Don't give in.

Press on!

Persevere.

Do whatever it takes. Whatever He asks of you.

Fight to the glorious finish, with every breath God gives you.

By His grace.

In His strength.

For His kingdom and glory.

Forever.

Amen.

The Bible talks about the "great cloud of witnesses," "an enormous crowd," those who've gone on before us, who surround us and cheer us on in our own race of faith. There's a long list of them in Hebrews 11–12, heroes of the faith. Who are your heroes or role models? Whose examples inspire you?

Who is your support team in your daily life? Who motivates, energizes, encourages, or inspires you?

think on it

Who are you setting an example for? Who are you mentoring or motivating? Who are you cheering on?

What kind of legacy do you want to leave for those who come after you? What life lessons do you want to share? What words of wisdom do you want to pass on?

Try using the format of a "six-word memoir" to tell your story. Say something about your journey so far—or how you would like to look back on your life—in six simple words.

Act on It

If you've ever signed up for any kind of a race or charity walk—or showed up to cheer someone else on—you've seen the signs, the homemade poster boards held up by friends and family to cheer the participants on to and over the finish line. Some of the messages are funny, some are sassy, some are sweet. But they all mean the same thing: "Keep going! You can do this! It will be worth it! We are proud of you!"

Draw your own sign in the space below with words that motivate or inspire you. Choose a favorite phrase or expression and illustrate it. Add a little color or a little glitter if you want to! Take a picture of it on your phone so you can pull it up anytime you need a little encouragement to rise and renew—and share it with others too!

I AM SPRINTING TOWARD THE ONLY GOAL THAT COUNTS: . . . TO HEAR GOD'S CALL *TO RESURRECTION LIFE FOUND EXCLUSIVELY* IN JESUS THE ANOINTED.

PHILIPPIANS 3:14 THE VOICE

And I'm so thankful that you joined me for this journey.

Now keep going!

Answer God's call to rise up in faith and
renew your spirit in Him each day.

A GUIDED PRAYER TO RISE UP AND RENEW

Dear God,

Your Word says, "Those who hope in the LORD will renew their strength. They will soar on wings like eagles; they will run and not grow weary, they will walk and not be faint" (Isaiah 40:31 NIV). I'm putting my hope in You today and asking for strength so that I will run toward the calling You've given me, I will rise to the challenges I'm facing, and my faith will be renewed by the power of Your Word and the Holy Spirit.

You are the God of all comfort, my help in times of trouble, my refuge and strength, and today I give you my thoughts, my words, and my actions, that they may bring glory to You.

In Jesus' name, amen.

YOUR PERSONAL PRAYER TO RISE UP AND RENEW

Dear God,

SUGGESTED BIBLE READINGS

The call to rise up and renew your faith is found throughout the Bible, and I want to offer you more places to go when you need strength and encouragement during challenging times. For the next thirty days, let these verses guide you on your journey toward a deeper connection with God.

Day 1. Exodus 14:1–14
Day 2. 1 Chronicles 16:7–36
Day 3. Psalm 1:1–6
Day 4. Psalm 23:1–6
Day 5. Psalm 27:1–14
Day 6. Psalm 46:1–11
Day 7. Psalm 84:1–12
Day 8. Ecclesiastes 3:12–14
Day 9. Isaiah 30:18
Day 10. Matthew 8:5–13
Day 11. Matthew 11:28–30
Day 12. Matthew 17:20
Day 13. Matthew 21:18–22
Day 14. Mark 10:13–16
Day 15. John 3:22–30
Day 16. John 15:18–25
Day 17. John 15:26–16:15
Day 18. John 17:20–26
Day 19. Acts 3:1–10
Day 20. Romans 10:9–17
Day 21. Romans 15:13
Day 22. 2 Corinthians 13:11
Day 23. Galatians 2:19–21
Day 24. 1 Thessalonians 3:12–13
Day 25. Hebrews 10:1–20
Day 26. Hebrews 11:1–40
Day 27. James 5:13–16
Day 28. 1 Peter 5:10–11
Day 29. 1 John 5:1–12
Day 30. Revelation 21:1–4

PHOTO CREDITS

page i: Anja Kaiser/Adobestock
pages ii, ix, 64, 66, 69, 204: jonbilous/Adobestock
page vii: Christine/Adobestock
page viii: NicoElNino/Adobestock
pages xii, 18, 21, 205: Art Wager/iStock
pages xv, 94, 96, 99: Syd/Adobestock
pages 10, 207, and back cover: Garrett Lobaugh
page 16: nullplus/Adobestock
page 22: Janature/Adobestock
pages xii, 24, 27, 201: mbbirdy/iStock
page 28: Galyna Andrushko/Adobestock
pages 30, 33: Dmitry/Adobestock
page 34: Danis/Adobestock
pages 36, 39: Rachel/Adobestock
page 40: Alice/Adobestock
pages 42, 45: sborisov/Adobestock
page 46: Sky Perth/Adobestock
pages 48, 51: abriendomundo/Adobestock
pages 52, 54, 57: Jeff/Adobestock
page 58: Tamara Sales/Adobestock
pages 60, 63: Simonova/Adobestock
pages 70, 72, 75: franz12/Adobestock
pages 76, 78, 81: Naglagla/Adobestock
page 82: Wirestock/Adobestock
pages 84, 87: Javier/Adobestock
page 88: Chloe/Adobestock
pages 90, 93, 206: Sundry Photography/Adobestock
page 100: Cavan/Adobestock
pages 102, 105: Khaleel/Adobestock
page 106: Georg/Adobestock
pages 108, 111: Jia Media/Adobestock
page 112: fesenko/Adobestock
pages 114, 117: Kevin/Adobestock
pages 118, 120, 123: Edie Layland/Adobestock
pages 124, 126, 129: jerzy/Adobestock
page 130: jon_chica/Adobestock
pages 132, 135: chones/Adobestock
page 136: Kemedo/Adobestock
pages 138, 141: Martina/Adobestock
pages 142, 144, 147, 174, 177: Jason/Adobestock
pages 148, 202: pozdeevvs/Adobestock
pages 150, 153: Sean Pavone Photo/Adobestock
pages 154, 156, 159, 160, 162, 165: Stefany Hedman/Adobestock
pages: 166, 168, 171, 208: Frank Peters/Adobestock
page 172: Ann Collins/Danita Delimont/Adobestock
pages 178, 180, 183: Drobot Dean/Adobestock
pages 184, 186, 189: DAVID/Adobestock
pages 190, 192, 195: Pixasquare/Adobestock
page 196: konoplizkaya/Adobestock
page 199: Anthony/Adobestock
page 203: woodsnorth/Adobestock

ABOUT THE AUTHOR

CANDACE CAMERON BURE is an actress, producer, and *New York Times* bestselling author. She is beloved by millions worldwide as everyone's big sister, D.J. Tanner, from the iconic television shows *Full House* and *Fuller House*. She has starred in more than 50 Christmas and cozy mystery movies, and is a former cohost of *The View*. She is CEO of CandyRock Entertainment and host of her self-titled podcast. Candace is both outspoken and passionate about her family and faith and continues to flourish in the entertainment industry as a role model to women of all ages.

www.candace.com

Candacecbure

Candacecameron

candacecameronb

ONLINE COMPANION COURSE

Want more? I created an online companion course for you! Scan the QR code with a mobile device to see how you can join me for exclusive Scripture readings, stories, and a community where you can connect with other readers.